200 meals for two

hamlyn | all colour cookbook

200 meals for two

Louise Blair

An Hachette UK Company
www.hachette.co.uk

First published in Great Britain in 2010 by Hamlyn,
a division of Octopus Publishing Group Ltd
Endeavour House, 189 Shaftesbury Avenue,
London WC2H 8JY

www.octopusbooks.co.uk

ISBN: 978-0-600-61931-4

A CIP catalogue record for this book is available
from the British Library

Printed and bound in China

2 3 4 5 6 7 8 9 10

Both metric and imperial measurements have been
given in all recipes. Use one set of measurements
only, and not a mixture of both.

Standard level spoon measurements are used in all recipes.
1 tablespoon = one 15 ml spoon
1 teaspoon = one 5 ml spoon

Ovens should be preheated to the specified temperature
– if using a fan-assisted oven, follow the manufacturer's
instructions for adjusting the time and the temperature.

Fresh herbs should be used unless otherwise stated.

Medium eggs should be used unless otherwise stated.

The Department of Health advises that eggs should not be
consumed raw. This book contains some dishes made with
raw or lightly cooked eggs. It is prudent for vulnerable
people such as pregnant and nursing mothers, invalids, the
elderly, babies and young children to avoid uncooked or
lightly cooked dishes made with eggs. Once prepared, these
dishes should be kept refrigerated and used promptly.

This book includes dishes made with nuts and nut
derivatives. It is advisable for those with known allergic
reactions to nuts and nut derivatives and those who
may be potentially vulnerable to these allergies to avoid
dishes made with nuts and nut oils. It is also prudent
to check the labels of pre-prepared ingredients for the
possible inclusion of nut derivatives.

contents

introduction

introduction

Most cookery books give recipes that are designed for four people, sometimes more, so when you are cooking for just two people what should you do?

Of course, some recipes are fairly easy to scale down by cutting ingredients in half, and many work well when you do this. But what do you do when it comes to halving ingredients such as a single egg or small amounts of herbs and spices? And what about cooking times? Should you halve them or leave them as for the original quantities of ingredients? The recipes in this book remove any guesswork and fiddly calculations, giving you plenty of delicious meals, from simple snacks to dishes for special occasions, all of which can easily be doubled or scaled up even further for more than four diners.

With just a little thought and planning, cooking for just two people can become a pleasure, rather than a chore. Don't make things unnecessarily difficult for yourself. Choose ingredients that are easy to come by and select recipes that are straightforward and quick to make and that, above all, taste delicious.

We are all aware of the healthy eating guidelines that the government and, increasingly, supermarkets are urging us to follow – though we should never forget that occasionally a little of what you fancy won't

do any harm. For day-to-day nutrition and good health, however, we should bear the following in mind and try to eat:

• More fruit and vegetables: our aim should be at least five portions a day. Try drinking a glass of fruit juice with breakfast and add some chopped fresh fruit to your cereal, and you'll be off to a great start.

• More starchy foods, such as rice, bread, pasta and potatoes. Carbohydrates should make up the biggest portion of your meal, followed by vegetables and protein. Slow-releasing, ('good') carbs, help to fill you up and to keep your energy levels constant throughout the day. Choose wholegrain varieties, wherever possible, as these contain more goodness.

• Less fat, salt and sugar. You should always check the labels on canned and packaged foods, but it's easy to overlook this when you're in a hurry. Obviously, cooking from scratch is the best way to ensure minimal salt and sugar content and be sparing about adding salt during cooking. Trimming any excess fat from cuts of meat and changing to lower-fat dairy products will help to reduce your fat intake.

• Some protein-rich foods, such as meat, eggs, pulses and fish: the recommendation is that we eat at least two portions of fish or shellfish each week, and one of these should be an oily fish, which is high in essential omega-3 fatty acid.

Healthy eating is also about using healthy cooking techniques and these can really help you to cut down on your fat intake, as well as maximize the nutritional value of your food. It might be worth investing in a steamer. They aren't very expensive and can be used for cooking all your vegetables, as well as some meat and fish. When you boil vegetables, much of the vitamin content is lost in the cooking liquid, whereas steaming retains it in the food. Another quick change is to grill or griddle food instead of frying it. Fish and meat just need a very light brush of oil before being placed on the griddle or under the grill.

menu planning

Take some time to prepare a weekly menu plan. This doesn't have to be set in stone, of course, and if your plans change it shouldn't be a problem to re-jig the menu and pop some things in the freezer to be used on another occasion.

Sensible planning means that if you want a roast meal then next day you use the leftover meat in a stir-fry or for a salad lunch. Broccoli cooked to accompany roast dinner one day could be used in Sausage and Broccoli Pasta (see pages 148–9) later in the week.

Where appropriate, double up quantities so that you can freeze individual portions to enjoy a couple of weeks later.

Remember to use your oven wisely: if you are making a casserole, roast potatoes at the same time or bake a dessert. This is a great way of saving energy and money.

Spend time writing a list for your weekly shop; you can keep these lists in a file or on your computer so that when you next plan a week with similar meals you have a list ready. Try to make the most of special offers if you can – extra meat and fish can be divided into portions for one and two and frozen for later use. A shopping list will help to prevent you from falling into the trap of buying things that you won't actually use.

Try to plan recipes that make the most of seasonal ingredients. Not only are vegetables and fruit cheaper when they are in season, but they often have a far better flavour. Also look out for locally produced goods that will be both fresh and flavoursome and will also help to keep down food miles. If you are lucky enough to have a local farmer's market or a street market near you, make the time to look around for really fresh and well-flavoured produce. Good-quality meat and fish then needs little adornment beyond a selection of steamed vegetables and perhaps some herb-flavoured butter (see pages 156–7) – nothing could be tastier or simpler.

store-cupboard essentials

You will soon find that there are some ingredients that you use every week and that you need to keep in stock.

• **Oils:** buy good-quality olive oil, which as well as being beneficial to your health is also a great staple for sauces, dressings and marinades. You will also need a vegetable or sunflower oil for cooking.

• **Mustards:** Dijon, wholegrain and English mustard will give depth of flavour to sauces and a kick to dressings and, of course, they can be used as an accompaniment to meats or in a sandwich.

• **Pasta:** perfect with a simple sauce for quick suppers; remember that different shapes suit different dishes. It's often easier to stick to one or two of your favourite shapes so that you aren't left with lots of half-used packets, each containing not quite enough for a meal.

• **Rice:** as with pastas there are several types to choose from, but basmati and risotto rices are always useful.

• **Sun-dried tomatoes:** chop these and add them to salads or pasta dishes.

• **Tomato purée:** use tomato purée or passata in sauces for pasta dishes, such as Bolognese. Keep jars in the refrigerator with the date you opened them written on so you don't forget.

• **Canned beans:** a great stand-by, canned beans – cannellini, kidney and borlotti beans, for example – don't need the long soaking and cooking of the dried equivalent, and they can be added to salads, soups and stews for vegetarians, giving a wonderful texture and taste. See, for example, Bean soup with guacamole (pages 64–5) and Italian bean & artichoke salad (pages 102–3).

• **Pine nuts:** quickly toasted, they are delicious additions to pastas and salads.

• **Sauces:** bottles of light and dark soy sauce and fish sauce (nam pla) are essential if you enjoy Eastern dishes of any kind.

• **Herbs and spices:** of course, fresh herbs have the best flavours, but not everyone has access to a herb garden or has the space to keep more than a few essentials growing on a windowsill. Packets or little jars of dried herbs, such as thyme, oregano and marjoram, and spices, such as chilli powder, garam masala, cumin, coriander and peppercorns, are useful, but remember to use them up because they lose their characteristic flavours over time.

• **Curry paste:** the ideal store-cupboard ingredient, a good-quality ready-made curry paste will allow you to stir-fry some vegetables with leftover meat or prawns. Simply stir in some coconut milk and serve with rice for a delicious and speedy supper.

refrigerator essentials

Your weekly shopping list will almost certainly include some, if not all, of the following:

• **Cheese:** a well-flavoured Cheddar cheese can be used for quick snacks, sandwiches and for grating into salads, while feta cheese can be crumbled into pasta dishes or used in salads. Parmesan cheese is not only essential for pasta and risottos but is also used in pesto and sauces.

• **Bacon:** chopped and cooked with a little garlic and tossed through pasta with a little single cream and some Parmesan cheese gives you a carbonara in minutes.

• **Fresh pasta and sauces:** although it is quick and easy to cook your own pasta and sauce, the ready-made packs can be prepared in minutes and are a good stand-by,

especially if you have some fresh Parmesan to grate over them.

• **Free-range eggs:** omelettes and frittatas are perfect meals for two people. Quick and easy to prepare and cook, they are the ideal way of using up leftover vegetables at the end of the week.

using your freezer

Before you put anything in your freezer make sure it's clearly labelled, and don't forget to include the date, so you know when it should be used by – things don't last forever, even in the freezer.

If you have time to cook in bulk, stock up your freezer to save yourself time and money. Shepherd pies, lasagnes, Bolognese sauce, chilli con carne, stews and casseroles, and even portions of mashed potato all freeze well, and these dishes can be complete life-savers when the cupboards are bare or you have unexpected visitors.

Frozen fruits and vegetables are always useful – frozen spinach, for example, can be quickly thawed and tossed through cooked pasta with a little cream, Parmesan cheese and a few toasted pine nuts. Frozen fruits can be popped into a blender with some fruit juice and yogurt to make an instant and filling smoothie. Freezing is also a great way to make the most of seasonal fruit and vegetables. Berries freeze particularly well and can be bought or picked when in abundance and then frozen for use during the winter months. The best way to freeze berries is to spread them in a single layer on a baking tray and then pop them in the freezer. Once they're solid you can transfer them into labelled bags. That way, they won't all freeze together in lumps and you'll be able to take out just a handful, as and when you need them.

basic recipes

Get really organized by having some pesto and homemade stock on standby.

homemade pesto

Although you can buy ready-made pesto in supermarkets and delicatessens, it is easy and quick to make at home. In a food processor or blender process together ½ garlic clove, 2 large handfuls of fresh basil, a handful of toasted pine nuts, 2 tablespoons grated Parmesan cheese and 6 tablespoons olive oil. Season to taste with salt and pepper. This will keep in a screw-top jar in the

can use leftover meat carcasses for chicken or beef stocks. Add some chopped carrots and onions to water. Add flavourings, such as peppercorns, bouquet garni, bay leafs and herbs, then bring to the boil and simmer for at least 1 hour. Leave to cool, then strain. The cooled stock can be frozen in portions and used as needed. See page 146 for a full version of a chicken stock recipe.

If making your own stock seems like too much effort or you really don't have the time, use one of the liquid stocks that are now available in supermarkets. Look out, too, for ready-made marinades in the herbs and spices sections of delicatessens and supermarkets and use them to add flavour to meat and fish before cooking.

refrigerator for 3–4 days. Toss the pesto through pasta or spread it over ciabatta or toast and top with vine-ripened tomatoes and torn mozzarella. Alternatively, combine it with a little mayonnaise (see pages 70–71) or crème fraîche, and stir through cooked new potatoes and griddled chicken or serve it with salad.

good-quality stock

Homemade stock is the basis of many recipes, and although you can buy cubes and powders to make up with water, a well-flavoured homemade stock will make a real difference to your cooking. There is a recipe for vegetable stock on pages 94–5, but you

brunch

blueberry french toasts

Serves **2**
Preparation time **5 minutes**
Cooking time **5 minutes**

2 **eggs**, beaten
100 ml (3½ fl oz) **single
  cream** or **milk**
¼ teaspoon **ground
  cinnamon**
2 **brioches**, cut in half
  horizontally
15 g (½ oz) **unsalted butter**

Blueberry compôte
300 g (10 oz) fresh
  blueberries
1 tablespoon **caster sugar**

Make the compôte. Put the blueberries and half the sugar into a small pan, place over a low heat and cook for 4–5 minutes until the berries are softened and beginning to ooze their juices. Set aside while you make the toasts.

Beat together the egg, cream or milk and cinnamon in a shallow bowl. Dip the brioches into the egg mixture and soak well.

Heat the butter in a nonstick frying pan, add the brioche and cook over a medium heat for 3–4 minutes, turning occasionally until browned all over. Serve with the blueberry compôte.

For mixed berries with chocolate toasts, make a compôte with 300 g (10 oz) frozen mixed berries and 1 tablespoon caster sugar as above. Replace the brioches with 2 pains au chocolat and cook them in the same way as the brioches.

mushroom & pancetta omelette

Serves **2**
Preparation time **15 minutes**
Cooking time **10–12 minutes**

1 tablespoon **olive oil**
175 g (6 oz) mixed **wild** or
   cup mushrooms, sliced
125 g (4 oz) **pancetta** or
   gammon steak, diced
3 tablespoons **crème fraîche**
4 teaspoons chopped **thyme**
4 **eggs**, separated
½ teaspoon **Dijon mustard**
20 g (¾ oz) **butter**
salt and **black pepper**

Heat the oil in a large frying pan, add the mushrooms and pancetta or gammon and fry for 5 minutes, stirring frequently, until golden. Stir in the crème fraîche and thyme, then remove the mixture from the pan and keep hot.

Wash and dry the pan. Whisk the egg whites into stiff, moist-looking peaks.

Mix together the egg yolks and mustard and season to taste with salt and pepper. Fold the mixture into the egg whites.

Heat the butter in the frying pan, add the egg mixture and cook over a medium heat for 3–4 minutes until the underside is golden. Quickly transfer the pan to a preheated hot grill, making sure that the handle is away from the heat, and cook for 2–3 minutes until the top is brown and the centre still slightly soft.

Spoon the mushroom and pancetta mixture over the omelette and fold in half. Serve immediately with a mixed salad.

For herb & ricotta omelette, whisk 4 egg whites until they form soft peaks. Fold through the egg yolks and 2 tablespoons chopped mixed herbs and 50 g (2 oz) ricotta. Season well with salt and pepper. Heat 25 g (1 oz) butter in a nonstick frying pan. Carefully add the egg mixture and cook for 3 minutes until the underside is golden. Transfer to a preheated grill as above and cook for 2–3 minutes.

breakfast muesli

Serves **2**

Preparation time **5 minutes**,
  plus soaking

125 g (4 oz) **jumbo oats**
1 tablespoon **pumpkin seeds**
1 tablespoon **sunflower seeds**
1 tablespoon **sesame seeds**
75 g (3 oz) ready-to-eat **dried apricots**, halved
50 g (2 oz) **dried cranberries**
250 ml (8 fl oz) **natural yogurt**

To serve
1 tablespoon **toasted almonds**, roughly chopped
2 tablespoons **clear honey**
milk (optional)

Mix together the oats, seeds, apricots, cranberries and yogurt. Chill in the refrigerator overnight.

Sprinkle the almonds over and serve the muesli drizzled with the honey and a little milk, if liked.

For tropical muesli, replace the cranberries with 50 g (2 oz) each of banana chips, dried mango, dried pineapple and 2 chopped dried figs. Omit the yogurt and serve with milk and a drizzle of clear honey.

beans & haloumi mushrooms

Serves **2**

Preparation time **10 minutes**

Cooking time **20 minutes**

4 large **portobello mushrooms**

2 **garlic cloves**, finely chopped

4 tablespoons chopped **mixed herbs**, such as thyme, rosemary, chives and parsley

6 tablespoons **olive oil**

415 g (13½ oz) can **baked beans**

few drops of **balsamic vinegar**

8 thin slices of **haloumi cheese**

black pepper

To serve

75 g (3 oz) **rocket leaves**

1 **pear**, cored and sliced

25 g (1 oz) **Parmesan cheese**, grated

Remove the stems from the mushrooms and place the caps, gill sides up, in an ovenproof dish. Sprinkle over half the garlic and herbs and season with black pepper. Drizzle with half the oil, place in a preheated oven, 200°C (400°F), Gas Mark 6, and roast for 10–15 minutes or until cooked through.

Mix the beans with a few drops of balsamic vinegar and heat through gently. Spoon the beans over the cooked mushrooms and arrange the slices of haloumi over the beans. Scatter over the reserved garlic and herbs and drizzle with the remaining oil. Put the dish under a preheated hot grill and cook for 2–3 minutes or until the haloumi is golden brown.

Divide the dish into individual portions of two mushrooms each and serve with a rocket, pear and Parmesan salad.

For bean & haloumi potato wedges, cut 2 large potatoes into 8 wedges each and parboil the pieces for 5 minutes. Drain thoroughly and put the potato wedges on a baking sheet. Drizzle over 1 tablespoon olive oil and cook under a preheated hot grill for 5–7 minutes until golden and tender. Mix 415 g (13½ oz) can baked beans with a few drops of balsamic vinegar, warm through and spoon over the potato wedges. Arrange 8 thin slices of haloumi cheese over the beans and return to the grill. Cook until bubbling and golden. Sprinkle over a tablespoon chopped parsley and serve.

baked eggs with salmon

Serves **2**
Preparation time **5 minutes**
Cooking time **10 minutes**

5 g (¼ oz) **unsalted butter**
125 g (4 oz) **smoked salmon**
 or **smoked trout**, cut into
 bite-sized pieces
2 large **eggs**
2 tablespoons **double cream**
1 tablespoon chopped **herbs**,
 such as chervil and chives
salt and **black pepper**

Grease 2 ramekins, each of 150 ml (¼ pint) capacity, with butter. Divide the salmon between the ramekins, then break in the eggs.

Mix together the cream and herbs and season to taste with salt and pepper. Pour into the ramekins and place them in a baking tin. Half-fill the tin with boiling water and transfer to a preheated oven, 200°C (400°F), Gas Mark 6, for about 10 minutes until the mixture is just set. Serve with triangles of crunchy fresh toast, if liked.

For baked eggs with ham, replace the salmon with 125 g (4 oz) sliced ham or Parma ham and break the eggs into the ramekins as before. Stir 1 teaspoon wholegrain mustard and 1 tablespoon snipped chives through the cream and add to the eggs. Cook as above until just set.

croque monsieur

Serves **2**
Preparation time **8 minutes**
Cooking time **5 minutes**

4 thick slices of **French
  country bread**
25 g (1 oz) **butter**, melted
25 g (1 oz) **Parmesan
  cheese**, finely grated
2 large slices of **roast ham**
125 g (4 oz) **Emmental
  cheese**, coarsely grated

Use a pastry brush to brush one side of each slice
of bread with the melted butter, then sprinkle with
the Parmesan.

Place 2 slices of bread on the worktop, with the
Parmesan-coated sides face down and top each with
a slice of ham and half the Emmental.

Top with the remaining 2 slices of bread, Parmesan-
coated sides on the outside, and toast in a sandwich
grill for 4–5 minutes or according to the manufacturer's
instructions until the bread is golden and crispy and
the Emmental is beginning to ooze from the sides.
Serve immediately.

For croque madame, make the sandwiches as above
and top each one with a fried egg.

eggs benedict with hollandaise

Serves **2**
Preparation time **10 minutes**
Cooking time **5 minutes**

2 large **eggs**
1 **English muffin**, halved
   horizontally and toasted
a little **butter**
4 slices of **Parma ham**
salt and **black pepper**

Hollandaise sauce
1 large **egg yolk**
1 teaspoon **lemon juice**
1 teaspoon **white wine
   vinegar**
50 g (2 oz) **butter**

Make the hollandaise sauce. Put the egg yolk into the small bowl of a food processor or a blender and season well with salt and pepper. Heat the lemon juice and vinegar in a small pan until just boiling. Switch on the processor and gradually add the vinegar mixture in a steady stream. Melt the butter in the pan and, with the processor switched on again, add this in a steady stream to give a smooth sauce.

Bring a large frying pan of water to the boil, then turn down the heat to a bare simmer. Break the eggs into the water and allow to cook very gently for 2 minutes. Remove from the pan with a slotted spoon.

Butter the muffins and top with the ham, a poached egg and a generous dollop of the sauce.

For salmon eggs benedict with tarragon hollandaise, replace the white wine vinegar with 1 teaspoon tarragon vinegar and stir 1 tablespoon chopped tarragon through the sauce. Cook the eggs in the same way, but use 50 g (2 oz) smoked salmon instead of the Parma ham.

brie & semi-dried tomato omelette

Serves **2**
Preparation time **5 minutes**
Cooking time **5 minutes**

4 large **eggs**, beaten
15 g (½ oz) **butter**
50 g (2 oz) **brie**, sliced
25 g (1 oz) **semi-dried
  tomatoes**
1 **spring onion**, sliced
salt and **black pepper**

Put the eggs in a bowl and beat them. Season to taste with salt and pepper.

Heat the butter in a large frying pan and add the egg mixture. Cook over a medium heat, gently pushing the mixture towards the centre of the pan and tipping the runny mixture to fill the spaces. When it is almost set remove from the heat and layer over the remaining ingredients. Fold over and serve immediately.

For smoked haddock, chive & crème fraîche omelette, mix together in a small bowl 100 g (3½ oz) poached and flaked smoked haddock, 1 tablespoon chopped chives and 1 tablespoon crème fraîche. Season with plenty of black pepper. Make the omelette as above and replace the filling with the smoked haddock mixture. Fold over and serve immediately.

ricotta & pear drizzle

Serves **2**
Preparation time **3 minutes**
Cooking time **1–2 minutes**

125 g (4 oz) **ricotta cheese**
4 thick slices of **all-butter
brioche**
1 small, sweet **dessert pear**,
  cored and finely sliced
50 ml (2 fl oz) **clear honey**,
  plus extra for drizzling

Spread the ricotta thickly over 2 slices of brioche and
fan out the pear slices over the top. Drizzle with the
honey and top with the remaining slices of brioche.

Toast in a sandwich grill for 1–2 minutes or according
to the manufacturer's instructions until the bread is
crisp and golden. Cut in half diagonally and serve
immediately, drizzled with extra honey.

For fig & mascarpone drizzle, beat together
2 tablespoons mascarpone cheese, 2 teaspoons
clear honey and a pinch of ground cinnamon. Lightly
toast one side of 4 thick slices of all-butter brioche.
Spread the mascarpone mixture over the untoasted
sides. Thinly slice a fresh fig and arrange the slices
over the mascarpone, scatter over 1 teaspoon
demerara sugar and cook under a preheated hot
grill for about 1 minute. Serve immediately.

omelette arnold bennett

Serves **2**

Preparation time **15 minutes**

Cooking time **10 minutes**

150 g (5 oz) **smoked haddock**

300 ml (½ pint) **fish stock**

2 tablespoons grated **Parmesan cheese**

6 **eggs**

2 tablespoons **cold water**

25 g (1 oz) **butter**

2 tablespoons **double cream**

salt and **black pepper**

Gently poach the haddock in the fish stock for 7–8 minutes or until just tender. Allow to cool then remove any skin and bones.

Flake the haddock, mix with the cheese and season to taste with salt and pepper. Put the eggs into a bowl and lightly beat with the water.

Melt the butter in an omelette pan and pour in the egg mixture. When the eggs begin to set, put the fish and cheese on top. While they are still liquid, pour over the cream then put the pan under a preheated hot grill for a few minutes until the top is golden brown. Do not fold the omelette but slide it on to a hot plate and serve immediately.

For bacon & leek omelette, make the omelette as above. In a frying pan melt 15 g (½ oz) butter and fry 1 finely sliced leek. Grill 4 rashers of bacon and chop. Scatter the cooked leek over the omelette with the chopped bacon and 25 g (1 oz) grated Gruyère cheese. Fold over the omelette and serve.

drop scones with fruit

Serves **2**
Preparation time **5 minutes**
Cooking time **5 minutes**

50 g (2 oz) **plain flour**
½ teaspoon **baking powder**
1 tablespoon **caster sugar**
25 g (1 oz) **dried fruit**, such
    as cranberries
1 **egg**, beaten
50 ml (2 fl oz) **milk**
15 g (½ oz) **unsalted butter**

Sift together the flour and baking powder and stir in the sugar and dried fruit. Add the egg and milk and beat to give a smooth batter.

Melt the butter in a frying pan. Add spoonfuls of the mixture to the pan and cook for about 1 minute or until lightly browned (you should have sufficient batter for 6 pancakes). Once the surface is covered in bubbles, turn over and cook until lightly browned.

Serve immediately with clear honey, if liked.

For Stilton cheese drop scones, replace the sugar and cranberries with 40 g (1½ oz) crumbled Stilton cheese and 2 finely sliced spring onions, which should be added to the bowl with the flour and baking powder. Prepare and cook the batter as above, making about 6 scones in all. Serve with butter.

cranberry granola

Serves **2**

Preparation time **10 minutes**

Cooking time **4–6 hours**

75 g (3 oz) **rolled oats**

25 g (1 oz) **dried cranberries**

½ tablespoon **sunflower oil**

1 tablespoon **clear honey**

skimmed milk or **low-fat**
   natural yogurt, to serve

Put all the ingredients in a warm mixing bowl and stir until the oats are covered evenly with the oil and honey.

Turn out onto a nonstick baking sheet, making sure that there are no lumps. Put in the bottom of a warm oven, 110°C (225°F), Gas Mark ¼, for 4–6 hours, stirring occasionally to prevent sticking or browning.

When crispy, remove and allow to cool. Serve with skimmed milk or low-fat yogurt. Store in an airtight container. The mixture will keep fresh for several days if kept free of moisture.

For apricot & seed granola, mix 25 g (1 oz) chopped dried apricots with the oats, sunflower oil and honey. Add 1 tablespoon each pumpkin seeds, sunflower seeds and sesame seeds. Cook and serve as above.

banana oat & almond muffins

Makes **12**
Preparation time **10 minutes**
Cooking time **20 minutes**

75 g (3 oz) **butter**, melted
2 tablespoons **clear honey**
1 **egg**, beaten
150 ml (¼ pint) **full-fat milk**
1 large **banana**, roughly
  chopped
175 g (6 oz) **self-raising flour**
75 g (3 oz) **oats**
1 teaspoon **baking powder**
25 g (1 oz) **ground almonds**
25 g (1 oz) **flaked almonds**

Mix together the butter, honey, egg and milk in a jug. Put the banana, flour, oats, baking powder and ground and flaked almonds in a large bowl. Pour in the milk mixture and quickly mix together all the ingredients to give a fairly lumpy mixture (this will give the muffins their lightness).

Line a 12-section muffin tin with paper cases and spoon in the batter. Bake in a preheated oven, 200°C (400°F), Gas Mark 6, for about 20 minutes until golden. Serve with butter and honey. Leftover muffins can be frozen or stored in an airtight container for three days.

For pear, apricot & almond muffins, replace the banana with a peeled and chopped pear, 2 fresh chopped apricots (or 4 ready-to-eat dried apricots) and add a few drops of almond essence to the mixture. Combine the fruit with the flour, oats, baking powder and almonds and quickly mix in the butter, honey, egg and milk as above. Cook as above.

stuffed mushrooms on toast

Serves **2**

Preparation time **5 minutes**

Cooking time **10–12 minutes**

1 tablespoon **olive oil**
4 large, **open-cap
  mushrooms**
150 g (2 oz) smoked **streaky
  bacon**, chopped
50 g (2 oz) **chorizo**, sliced
15 g (½ oz) **butter**
1 **garlic clove**, crushed
  (optional)
1 tablespoon chopped
  parsley

Heat the oil in a large frying pan. Lightly fry the mushrooms in the oil for 2–3 minutes, turning once.

Put the mushrooms, gill side up, in an ovenproof dish (there is no need to remove the stalks). Fry the bacon and chorizo in the butter and garlic (if using) until bacon has browned. Stir in the parsley.

Spoon the bacon mixture into the mushrooms and bake in a preheated oven, 200°C (400°F), Gas Mark 6, for 10–12 minutes or until the mushrooms are cooked through. Serve with thick slices of granary or wholewheat toast.

For spinach-stuffed mushrooms, omit the bacon and chorizo. Heat the butter and fry ½ small onion and the garlic for 2–3 minutes. Add 3 large handfuls of baby leaf spinach and a good grating of nutmeg and cook briefly until the spinach has just wilted. Put the mixture in the mushrooms and top with a grating of fresh Parmesan cheese. Cook as above.

berry breakfast

Serves **2**

Preparation time **15 minutes**, plus chilling

150 ml (½ pint) **Greek yogurt**
1 tablespoon **clear honey**
175 g (6 oz) **raspberries**
15 g (½ oz) **porridge oats**

Put the yogurt in a large bowl and fold in the honey.

Divide one-third of the raspberries between 2 serving glasses. Cover with half the yogurt mixture. Scatter over some of the oats and more raspberries, dividing them evenly among the glasses.

Repeat the layers, finishing with oats and a few raspberries. Chill in the refrigerator for 30 minutes before serving.

For mango breakfast, purée the flesh of 1 large, ripe mango. Add the mango instead of the raspberries to the yogurt, honey and oats as above.

kedgeree

Serves **2**
Preparation time **10 minutes**
Cooking time **15 minutes**

200 g (7 oz) **smoked haddock**
200 ml (7 fl oz) **milk**
1 **bay leaf**
2 teaspoons **vegetable oil**
1 small **onion**, chopped
125 g (4 oz) **basmati rice**
½ teaspoon **curry powder**
2 **hard-boiled eggs**, roughly chopped
1 tablespoon chopped **parsley**

Put the haddock in a small saucepan with the milk and bay leaf, simmer for 3 minutes or until just cooked and remove the fish from the milk, reserving the milk. Flake the fish and set aside.

Heat the oil in a medium-sized frying pan. Add the onion and fry for 3 minutes. Add the rice and curry powder and fry for a further minute.

Make the reserved milk up to 250 ml (8 fl oz) with water and pour it over the rice. Cover and cook for 12 minutes until the rice is cooked and fluffy. Add the remaining ingredients and the flaked haddock, stir to combine and serve.

For mackerel & pea kedgeree, flake 200 g (7 oz) peppered smoked mackerel instead of the haddock and use 250 ml (8 fl oz) water to cook the rice. Add 100 g (3½ oz) frozen peas to the rice 3 minutes before the end of cooking time.

gravlax & cream cheese bagels

Serves **2**

Preparation time **14 minutes**

Cooking time **14–16 minutes**

2 **poppy and sesame seed bagels**, cut in half horizontally

125 g (4 oz) **cream cheese**

175 g (6 oz) **gravlax**, finely sliced

2 tablespoons chopped **chives**

black pepper, plus extra to serve

Put the bagels, cut side down, on a sandwich grill. Without closing the lid, leave them to toast for 2–3 minutes until golden. Remove from the grill.

Spread the bases with the cream cheese and then top with the gravlax. Scatter the chopped chives over the bagel and season with black pepper.

Top with the bagel lids and return to the sandwich grill. Lower the top plate and toast for 2–3 minutes or according to the manufacturer's instructions until golden and crispy. Serve immediately with a sprinkling of black pepper.

For salt beef & pickle bagels, cut 2 bagels in half horizontally and toast them on both sides. Layer 2 of the bagel halves with 50 g (2 oz) sliced salt beef and 2 sliced pickled gherkins. Mix together 1 tablespoon light crème fraîche and 1 teaspoon Dijon mustard and spoon the mixture over the beef and gherkins. Garnish with watercress and top with the other bagel halves.

big raspberry muffins

Makes **6**
Preparation time **5 minutes**
Cooking time **15–20 minutes**

200 g (7 oz) **plain flour**
75 g (3 oz) **caster sugar**
2 tablespoons **ground almonds**
2 teaspoons **baking powder**
grated rind of **1 lemon**
150 ml (¼ pint) **buttermilk**
1 **egg**, beaten
50 g (2 oz) **butter**, melted
150 g (5 oz) fresh or frozen **raspberries**

Mix together the flour, sugar, ground almonds, baking powder and lemon rind in a large bowl. In a separate bowl mix together the remaining ingredients, then fold into the flour mixture to give a slightly lumpy texture.

Spoon the batter into 6 large muffin paper cases set in a muffin tin and cook in a preheated oven, 180°C (350°F), Gas Mark 4, for 15–20 minutes until golden and risen. These muffins can be frozen or stored in an airtight tin.

For blackcurrant crunch muffins, make the batter as above, replacing the raspberries with 150 g (5 oz) fresh blackcurrants. Spoon the batter into 6 muffin paper cases and sprinkle the top of the uncooked muffins with 1 tablespoon chopped hazelnuts and 1 tablespoon demerara sugar. Cook as above.

fruit & nut bars

Makes **8**
Preparation time **10 minutes**
Cooking time **15 minutes**

100 g (3½ oz) **butter**, plus
 extra for greasing
4 tablespoons **maple syrup**
2 tablespoons **soft light
 brown sugar**
150 g (5 oz) **jumbo oats**
100 g (3½ oz) **oatmeal**
50 g (2 oz) **mixed nuts**,
 chopped
150 g (5 oz) **mixed dried
 fruit**, such as figs, dates,
 ready-to-eat apricots and
 cranberries, chopped
2 tablespoons **sunflower
 seeds**

Lightly grease a 20 cm (8 inch) square, nonstick baking tin and line the base with nonstick baking paper. In a saucepan melt the butter, syrup and sugar together. Stir in all the remaining ingredients except the sunflower seeds, then press the mixture into the prepared tin.

Sprinkle over the sunflower seeds, then bake in a preheated oven, 200°C (400°F), Gas Mark 6, for 15 minutes or until golden. Cut into 8 bars, leave to cool, then serve. These bars can be stored in an airtight container for up to one week.

For speedy flapjacks, melt 175 g (6 oz) unsalted butter with 175 g (6 oz) dark brown sugar in a saucepan. Remove from the heat and stir through 250 g (8 oz) square jumbo oats. Press the mixture into a lined and greased 20 cm (8 in) baking tin and cook in a preheated oven, 180°C (350°F), Gas Mark 4, for 15 minutes. Cut into 12 bars and leave to cool.

hot vanilla

Serves **2**

Preparation time **5 minutes**, plus standing

Cooking time **2 minutes**

300 ml (½ pint) **milk**

125 g (4 oz) **white chocolate**, chopped

½ teaspoon **vanilla extract**

unsweetened **cocoa powder**, for sprinkling

vanilla pod, to decorate (optional)

Pour the milk into a saucepan and bring it almost to the boil. Remove the pan from the heat and tip in the chocolate. Leave to stand for 2–3 minutes, stirring frequently, until the chocolate has melted.

Add the vanilla extract to the saucepan. Beat with a balloon whisk or an immersion blender until the milk is smooth and topped with a thick foam.

Pour the hot milk between 2 mugs and serve sprinkled with cocoa. Decorate with a vanilla pod, if liked.

For hot mint chocolate, heat 300 ml (½ pint) milk and add 125 g (4 oz) chopped plain dark chocolate. Leave, stirring, until the chocolate has melted, add peppermint essence to taste (about ½ teaspoon) and whisk as above.

light bites

vietnamese crab lettuce rolls

Serves **2**
Preparation time **10 minutes**

2 x 170 g (5½ oz) cans **crab**,
   drained, or the equivalent
   weight **fresh crab**
1 **red chilli**, deseeded and
   finely chopped
handful of **fresh coriander**,
   chopped
1 tablespoon chopped **mint**
grated rind and juice of **1 lime**
1 cm (½ inch) **fresh root**
   ginger, finely grated
4 **iceberg lettuce leaves**,
   halved

Chilli dipping sauce
1 teaspoon **soft brown sugar**
1 tablespoon **rice vinegar**
juice of ½ **lime**
1 teaspoon **soy sauce**
1 **red chilli**, finely chopped
1 **spring onion**, finely sliced

Mix together the crab, chilli, coriander, mint, lime rind
and juice and the ginger in a bowl.

Spoon equal amounts of the mixture onto the lettuce
leaves. Roll them up and set them aside.

Make the dipping sauce. In a small bowl mix together
the sugar, vinegar, lime juice and soy sauce until the
sugar has dissolved. Stir in the chilli and spring onion.

Serve the crab lettuce rolls with the chilli sauce for
dipping in a separate dish.

For crab & noodle lettuce rolls, cook 100 g (3½ oz)
rice noodles in boiling water according to the
instructions on the packet. Leave the noodles to cool,
then combine them with the crab, coriander, mint,
lemon rind and juice and ginger as above. Wrap this
mixture in halved iceberg lettuce leaves and serve with
the chilli dipping sauce.

asparagus and fontina toastie

Serves **2**

Preparation time **5 minutes**

Cooking time **3–4 minutes**

125 g (4 oz) trimmed **asparagus spears**

4 thin slices of **Black Forest ham**

75 g (3 oz) **fontina cheese**, grated

small handful of **rocket**

2 **vine-ripened tomatoes**, sliced

4 slices of **sourdough bread**

2 tablespoons **olive oil**

2 teaspoons **balsamic vinegar**

Steam the asparagus in a steamer for 3–4 minutes so that it is still quite firm. Leave to cool.

Arrange the ham, grated fontina, rocket, asparagus and tomatoes over 2 slices of sourdough bread. Drizzle with the oil and balsamic vinegar and top with the remaining slices of bread.

Toast the sandwiches in a sandwich grill for about 3–4 minutes or according to the manufacturer's instructions until the bread is golden and the cheese has melted. Serve immediately.

For salmon & cream cheese toastie, spread 25 g (1 oz) cream cheese over 2 slices of sourdough bread. Arrange 40 g (1½ oz) smoked salmon over the cheese, squeeze over a little lemon juice and season well with black pepper. Top each with another slice of sourdough bread and cook in a sandwich grill as above.

trout pâté & sesame biscuits

Serves **2**

Preparation time **15 minutes**,
  plus chilling

Cooking time **10 minutes**

Biscuits

100 g (3½ oz) **plain flour**

50 g (2 oz) **butter**

2 tablespoons grated
  Parmesan cheese

1 **egg yolk**, beaten

1 tablespoon **sesame seeds**

Pâté

125 g (7 oz) **hot-smoked
  trout fillets**

1 tablespoon **capers**, drained

2 tablespoons **crème fraîche**

1 teaspoon **horseradish
  sauce**

1 teaspoon chopped **dill**

Put the flour and butter in a bowl and rub together with your fingertips until the mixture resembles breadcrumbs. Stir in the Parmesan and enough egg yolk to bring the mixture together into a dough.

Roll out the pastry on a lightly floured surface, brush with the remaining egg and sprinkle over the sesame seeds. Cut the dough into about 20 biscuits with a biscuit cutter, transfer to nonstick baking sheets and bake in a preheated oven, 200°C (400°F), Gas Mark 6, for about 10 minutes. Leave to cool on a wire rack.

Put the trout, capers, crème fraîche, horseradish and dill in a food processor or blender and process for about 10 seconds until the ingredients are combined but still retain some texture. Chill for about 30 minutes, then serve with the biscuits. Uneaten biscuits can be stored in an airtight tin for a few days.

For roasted pepper pâté, put a large red pepper under a hot grill and cook until blackened. Transfer to a bowl and cover with clingfilm. Leave to cool, then remove the skin and finely chop the flesh. Beat the pepper flesh into 100 g (3½ oz) cream cheese and 1 tablespoon green pesto. Transfer the pâté to a bowl, chill for 30 minutes and serve with sesame biscuits.

bean soup with guacamole

Serves **2**
Preparation time **10 minutes**
Cooking time **15 minutes**

1 teaspoon **olive oil**
1 **onion**, chopped
1 **garlic clove**, crushed
1 **red chilli**, deseeded and
    chopped
400 g (13 oz) can **mixed
    beans**, rinsed and drained
220 g (7½ oz) can **chopped
    tomatoes**
300 ml (½ pint) **vegetable
    stock** (see pages 94–5 for
    homemade)
salt and **black pepper**

Guacamole
1 **avocado**, skinned and
    stoned
2 **spring onions**, finely sliced
2 **tomatoes**, chopped
1 tablespoon chopped **fresh
    coriander**
juice of ½ **lime**

Make the guacamole. Roughly chop the avocado flesh and mash it together with the spring onions, tomatoes, coriander and lime juice. Set aside.

Heat the oil in a medium saucepan. Add the onion, garlic and chilli and fry for 2–3 minutes or until softened. Add the beans, tomatoes and stock, bring to the boil and simmer for 10 minutes.

Transfer three-quarters of the soup to a food processor or blender and process until almost smooth. Add to the reserved soup and stir to combine. Season to taste with salt and pepper and warm through.

Serve the soup with the guacamole and tortilla crisps.

For smoked bacon & bean soup with guacamole,
add 50 g (2 oz) chopped smoked streaky bacon to the saucepan with the onion, garlic and chilli and cook for 2–3 minutes. Continue as above. Garnish with a spoonful of crème fraîche and serve with the guacamole.

crunchy thai-style salad

Serves **2**
Preparation time **10 minutes**

2 carrots
1 courgette
½ small **red cabbage**, finely
   shredded
1 **yellow pepper**, cored,
   deseeded and thinly sliced
4 **spring onions**, finely sliced
2 tablespoons chopped **fresh
   coriander**
150 g (5 oz) **rice noodles**

Dressing
1 **red chilli**, deseeded and
   chopped
4 tablespoons **fish sauce**
   (nam pla)
grated rind and juice of **1 lime**
2 tablespoons **caster sugar**

Use a potato peeler to shred the carrots and courgette
into fine slices. Toss together the sliced vegetables with
the cabbage, pepper, spring onions and coriander.

Cook the noodles in boiling water according to the
instructions on the packet, drain and leave to cool.

Make the dressing by whisking together the chilli, fish
sauce, lime rind and juice and sugar in a small bowl.

Mix the noodles with the vegetables. Toss the dressing
through the salad and serve.

For crunchy coleslaw salad, toss together the sliced
carrots, courgette, cabbage, pepper and spring onions
as above. In a separate bowl beat together 1 tablespoon
crème fraîche, 1 tablespoon mayonnaise, 1 teaspoon
mustard and a good squeeze of lemon juice. Stir this
dressing into the vegetables, scatter over 25 g (1 oz)
coriander and serve.

lamb tortilla wraps

Serves **2**

Preparation time **5 minutes**

Cooking time **8–10 minutes**

1 teaspoon **olive oil**

1 **garlic clove**, finely chopped

1 small **onion**, finely chopped

125 g (4 oz) lean **lamb leg steaks**, cut into small strips

50 g (2 oz) **mushrooms**, finely chopped

½ small **red pepper**, cored, deseeded and sliced

1 tablespoon chopped **parsley**

1 tablespoon chopped **mint**

50 g (2 oz) **basmati rice**, cooked

2 tablespoons **lemon juice**

2 tablespoons **Greek yogurt**

1 tablespoon **mint sauce**

4 flour **tortillas** or **flatbreads**

5 cm (2 inches) **cucumber**, cut into strips

Make the filling. Heat the oil in a nonstick wok or frying pan and cook the garlic, onion and lamb strips for 3–4 minutes until brown. Add the mushrooms and pepper and cook for 2–3 minutes. Stir in the herbs, rice and lemon juice. Heat for a further 1–2 minutes.

Mix together the yogurt and mint sauce in a bowl.

Assemble the wraps. Lay the flour tortillas on a clean work surface. Spread a dessertspoon of the yogurt mixture over each tortilla, top with a large spoonful of the filling and a few strips of cucumber.

Fold up to make neat rolls and serve immediately with a rocket salad.

For chicken tortilla wraps, use either 250 g (8 oz) chicken strips or the same weight of boneless, skinless chicken breasts, cut into strips. Cook the garlic and onions as above. Add the chicken to the pan and stir-fry until cooked through. Add the vegetables and remaining ingredients to the pan. Make the tortillas as above and serve with mayonnaise or salsa verde (see page 100–1 for homemade).

tiger prawns & watercress mayo

Serves **2**

Preparation time **15 minutes**

3 tablespoons **mayonnaise**

large handful of **watercress**,
   plus extra to serve

2 **gherkins**, roughly chopped

grated rind and juice of
   ½ **lemon**

250 g (8 oz) **tiger prawns**,
   cooked

salt and **black pepper**

Put the mayonnaise, watercress, gherkins and lemon rind and juice into a food processor or blender and process until almost smooth. Season to taste with salt and pepper.

Toss the prawns in the dressing to coat and serve with fresh, crusty bread and extra watercress.

For chicken & pesto mayo, stir 1 tablespoon pesto through 2 tablespoons mayonnaise. Toss 2 cooked and chopped chicken breasts through the dressing and serve with pitta bread.

walnut & pear salad

Serves **2**

Preparation time **10 minutes**

1 tablespoon **olive oil**

200 g (7 oz) **ciabatta**, torn
  into bite-sized pieces

1 **cos lettuce**, torn into
  bite-sized pieces

1 large, ripe **pear**, cored and
  finely sliced

25 g (1 oz) toasted **walnuts**,
  roughly chopped

Dressing

3 tablespoons **crème fraîche**

50 g (2 oz) **Stilton cheese**,
  crumbled

1 **anchovy**, drained and
  chopped

2 tablespoons **water**

black pepper

Drizzle the oil over the ciabatta pieces, then toast the bread under a preheated hot grill until golden all over. Toss the croutons together with the lettuce, pear and walnuts.

Make the dressing. Mix together the crème fraîche, Stilton, anchovy and water in a small bowl and season with plenty of pepper.

Spoon the dressing over the salad and serve.

For chicken & pancetta salad, prepare all the salad ingredients as above but omit the pear. Heat 1 teaspoon olive oil in a frying pan. Add 1 thinly sliced chicken breast and fry for 3–4 minutes. Set aside. Add 4 slices of pancetta to the pan and cook for about 1 minute until crisp. Mix the chicken with the salad and serve with the pancetta on top.

toasted peanut & wild rice salad

Serves **2**
Preparation time **5 minutes**
Cooking time **30 minutes**

125 g (4 oz) **basmati rice**
25 g (1 oz) **wild rice**
1 bunch of **spring onions**,
  chopped
125 g (4 oz) **sultanas**
125 g (4 oz) toasted **peanuts**
4 tablespoons **balsamic
  vinegar**
1 tablespoon **sunflower oil**

Cook both types of rice according to the instructions on the packets. Rinse in cold water and drain thoroughly.

Mix together the cooked rice, spring onions, sultanas and peanuts in a large bowl.

Pour the vinegar and oil into a small bowl and whisk together, then stir the dressing into the rice mixture. Serve with a salad of crisp green leaves.

For trout & wild rice salad, cook the rice as above and add the spring onions, sultanas and peanuts. Flake 150 g (5 oz) smoked trout fillet and stir through the rice salad with 50 g (2 oz) chopped watercress. Dress and serve as above.

aubergine pâté

Serves **2**
Preparation time **10 minutes**
Cooking time **30–40 minutes**

2 **aubergines**, cubed
2 **garlic cloves**, sliced
2 tablespoons **olive oil**
1 teaspoon **cumin seeds**
pinch of **chilli flakes**
1 tablespoon chopped **fresh coriander**
salt and **black pepper**

Put the aubergines in a baking tin and add the garlic. Drizzle over the oil and then sprinkle over the cumin seeds and chilli flakes. Season well with salt and pepper.

Cook in a preheated oven, 200°C (400°F), Gas Mark 6, for 35–40 minutes until tender and golden.

Transfer the mixture to a food processor or blender and process for a few seconds so that the mixture still has some texture. Leave to cool, then stir through the chopped coriander. Serve with toasted pitta bread.

For Mediterranean pâté, cook 1 aubergine and 1 chopped yellow pepper with garlic as above, sprinkling the leaves from a sprig of lemon thyme over the olive oil instead of the cumin and chilli flakes. Leaves to cool then transfer to a food processor or blender and process with 3 tablespoons cream cheese to make a smooth mixture.

cheesy tortillas with tuna salsa

Serves **2**
Preparation time **10 minutes**
Cooking time **5 minutes**

300 g (10 oz) fresh **tuna**, cut
    into small cubes
1 **avocado**, peeled, stoned
    and chopped
1 large **tomato**, chopped
½ **green chilli**, deseeded and
    chopped
large handful of **watercress**,
    chopped
salt and **black pepper**

Tortillas
2 large **flour tortillas**
50 g (2 oz) **mozzarella**
    cheese, finely sliced
2 **spring onions**, sliced
1 tablespoon chopped **fresh**
    coriander

Mix together the tuna, avocado, tomato, chilli and
watercress in a non-metallic dish and set aside for
10 minutes.

Meanwhile, heat a large frying pan. Place one tortilla
on a chopping board. Layer the mozzarella, spring
onions and coriander on top of the tortilla. Put the
other tortilla on top, press down a little and transfer to
the frying pan. Cook for 1 minute, then turn over and
cook for a further minute. Cut into wedges and serve
with the tuna salsa.

**For cheesy tortillas with goats' cheese & red
pepper salsa**, roughly chop 150 g (5 oz) goats'
cheese. Halve, core and deseed 1 red pepper and
roughly chop the flesh. Toss the cheese and pepper
together with 1 chopped avocado, 1 chopped large
tomato, ½ green chilli, deseeded and chopped, and a
large handful of watercress. Serve with cheesy tortillas
prepared as above.

chicken & sweet potato soup

Serves **2**

Preparation time **10 minutes**

Cooking time **15 minutes**

2 teaspoons **olive oil**

1 small **onion**, chopped

1 **garlic clove**, crushed

1 **red chilli**, deseeded and
chopped

1 large **sweet potato**, peeled
and cubed

1 large boneless, skinless
chicken breast, chopped

1 x 400 g (13 oz) can
coconut milk

600 ml (1 pint) **chicken stock**
(see pages 13 and 146)

1 tablespoon chopped **fresh
coriander**

salt

Heat the oil in a nonstick frying pan. Add the onion,
garlic and chilli and fry for 3 minutes until softened.
Add the sweet potato and chicken and continue to fry
for 2–3 minutes until the chicken is coloured all over.

Add the coconut milk and stock to the pan, bring to
the boil, cover and simmer for 15 minutes until the
potato is tender.

Transfer to a food processor or blender and process
until smooth. Season to taste with salt, stir through the
chopped coriander and serve.

For spiced butternut squash soup, cook the onion,
garlic and chilli as above, but omit the chicken and
replace the sweet potato with 1 medium peeled and
chopped butternut squash. Add the coconut milk and
300 ml (½ pint) vegetable stock (see pages 94–5 for
homemade) instead of the chicken stock. Bring to the
boil and finish as above.

herbed citrus chicken salad

Serves **2**

Preparation time **20 minutes**,
   plus marinating

Cooking time **10–15 minutes**

2 boneless, skinless **chicken
   breasts**

150 g (5 oz) shredded **cos
   lettuce**

150 g (5 oz) shredded
   radicchio

½ large **avocado**, stoned,
   peeled and thinly sliced

1 tablespoon chopped **fresh
   coriander**

Lemon cumin dressing

2 tablespoons **lemon juice**

½ teaspoon **soy sauce**

1 teaspoon **ground cumin**

6 tablespoons **olive oil**

Orange & coriander marinade

2 tablespoons **olive oil**

½ tablespoon **lemon juice**

½ tablespoon **orange juice**

2 **garlic cloves**, chopped

½ teaspoon **ground coriander**

½ teaspoon **ground cumin**

¼ teaspoon **cinnamon**

Make the marinade. Mix together all the ingredients in a small bowl. Put the chicken breasts in a non-metallic dish and, reserving 2 tablespoons for basting, pour the rest of the marinade over the chicken, coating it thoroughly. Cover and refrigerate for 20 minutes.

Meanwhile, make the dressing. Mix together the lemon juice, soy sauce, cumin and oil in a bowl. Set aside.

Remove the chicken from the marinade, reserving the marinade, and place it on a foil-lined baking sheet. Put the baking sheet on a rack and place it about 15 cm (6 inches) below a preheated grill. Cook the chicken, turning occasionally and brushing it with the reserved marinade, for about 10 minutes or until a skewer will easily go into the chicken and the juices run clear.

Put the shredded cos and radicchio lettuces in a large bowl. Toss with 1–2 tablespoons of the dressing then arrange on a large platter. Cut the chicken breasts into 1 cm (½ inch) slices and set them on the lettuce.

Garnish with the avocado slices. Pour the remaining dressing over, sprinkle with chopped coriander and serve.

For herbed citrus tofu salad, cut 200 g (7 oz) tofu into thin slices. Make the marinade as above and marinate the tofu for at least 20 minutes. Cook the tofu under a preheated hot grill for 2–3 minutes. Prepare the salad as above and dress with lemon cumin dressing. Toss the salad and dressing together to mix, add the tofu and serve, garnished with chopped fresh coriander.

lentil & tomato salad with egg

Serves **2**

Preparation time **5 minutes**

Cooking time **5 minutes**

2 teaspoons **olive oil**

4 **spring onions**, sliced

1 **garlic clove**, crushed

400 g (13 oz) can **puy lentils** or **green lentils**, rinsed and drained

150 g (5 oz) **cherry tomatoes**, halved

1 tablespoon chopped **parsley**

1 tablespoon **balsamic vinegar**

2 **eggs**

Heat the oil in a nonstick frying pan. Add the spring onions and garlic and fry for 1 minute. Add the lentils, tomatoes, parsley and vinegar and warm through.

Meanwhile, bring a large pan of lightly salted water to the boil. Stir the water to make a gentle 'whirlpool' and crack in an egg, allowing the white to wrap around the yolk. Cook for 3 minutes, remove from the pan and cook the other egg in the same way.

Serve the eggs on a bed of lentils with some crusty bread to mop up the juices.

For chorizo & rice salad with egg, replace the lentils with 300 g (10 oz) cooked basmati and wild rice (buy ready-mixed and cook according to the instructions on the packet). Continue as above and serve topped with 8 slices of grilled chorizo and a poached egg on each serving.

stilton welsh rarebit

Serves **2**
Preparation time **5 minutes**
Cooking time **5 minutes**

15 g (½ oz) **butter**
4 **spring onions**, sliced
100 g (4 oz) **Stilton cheese**,
  crumbled
1 **egg yolk**
a little **milk**
2 slices of **granary bread**,
  lightly toasted
2 slices of **bacon**, grilled

Heat the butter in a small saucepan and fry the spring onions for 2–3 minutes until softened. Leave to cool, then mix with the Stilton and egg yolk, adding enough milk to make a spreadable mixture.

Spread the mixture over the toast and cook under a preheated hot grill for about 2 minutes until golden and bubbling. Serve topped with the grilled bacon.

For Cheddar rarebit, use 75 g (3 oz) grated Cheddar cheese instead of the Stilton and add ½ teaspoon English mustard to the mixture before spreading it over the toast. Grill under a preheated hot grill and serve as above.

chilli bean con carne

Serves **2**
Preparation time **30 minutes**
Cooking time **55 minutes**

1 tablespoon **olive oil**
1 small **onion**, finely chopped
1 **garlic clove**, crushed
250 g (8 oz) **minced beef**
1 tablespoon **tomato purée**
1 large **red chilli**, chopped
½ teaspoon **hot chilli powder**
1 teaspoon dried **mixed
 herbs**
200 g (7 oz) can **chopped
 tomatoes**
225 g (7½ oz) can **baked
 beans**
black pepper

To serve
100 ml (3½ fl oz) **soured
 cream**
1 tablespoon chopped **flat-
 leaf parsley**
50 g (2 oz) **Cheddar cheese**,
 grated
jalapeño peppers (optional)

Make the chilli. Heat the oil in a large pan, add the onion and garlic and cook over a medium heat for 5 minutes or until softened. Increase the heat to high and add the minced beef. Fry, stirring, for 5 minutes or until browned all over.

Stir in the tomato purée, chilli, chilli powder and mixed herbs and continue to cook for 5 minutes. Add the tomatoes and baked beans, bring to the boil, cover and simmer for 30 minutes.

Transfer the chilli to a serving bowl and top with soured cream. Garnish with pepper and chopped parsley and serve with cheesy scones (see below) and separate bowls of grated cheese and jalapeño peppers, if liked.

For scones, to serve as an accompaniment, mix together 250 g (8 oz) plain flour and 2 teaspoons baking powder in a large bowl. Rub in 75 g (3 oz) diced butter and add 50 g (2 oz) mature, grated Cheddar cheese. Make a well in the centre and pour in 1 beaten egg and 50 ml (2 fl oz) milk. Use a knife to mix the dough until it comes together. Turn out the dough on to a lightly floured surface and roll it out to about 5 mm (¼ inch) thick. Cut out 8 rounds, each 5 cm (2 inches) in diameter, and place them on a baking sheet. Brush the tops with a little milk and bake in a preheated oven, 200°C (400°F), Gas Mark 6, for 12 minutes or until they sound hollow when tapped.

spinach & feta tarts

Makes **4**

Preparation time **10 minutes**, plus chilling

Cooking time **25 minutes**

Pastry

200 g (7 oz) **plain flour**

100 g (3½ oz) cold **butter**, diced

about 100 ml (3½ fl oz) **cold water**

Filling

150 g (5 oz) **baby leaf spinach**

150 ml (¼ pint) **crème fraîche**

1 **egg**, beaten

50 g (2 oz) **feta cheese**, crumbled

grated **nutmeg**

black pepper

Sift the flour into a large bowl, add the butter and rub in with your fingertips until the mixture resembles fine breadcrumbs. Add enough cold water to make a ball. Bring the dough together, wrap in clingfilm and chill for 30 minutes.

Divide the pastry into 4, roll out each piece and use it to line 4 lightly greased tartlet tins, each 9 cm (3½ inches) across. Bake blind (i.e. bake the empty cases without filling) in a preheated oven, 200°C (400°F), Gas Mark 6, for 5 minutes. Then remove the cases, but leave the oven on.

Meanwhile, put the spinach in a large colander, pour over boiling water to wilt the leaves, then squeeze out any liquid. Divide the spinach among the pastry cases. Whisk together the crème fraîche and egg and season well with grated nutmeg and black pepper. Stir through the feta. Pour the mixture into the pastry cases (still in their tartlet tins) and cook for 15–20 minutes or until golden and puffy. Serve with a side salad.

For trout & asparagus tarts, make the pastry cases as above. Halve 8 trimmed asparagus spears and simmer in boiling water for 1 minute, then drain. Arrange the asparagus in the tartlet cases with 75 g (3 oz) flaked smoked trout. Mix together 150 ml (¼ pint) crème fraîche and 1 egg as above and pour the mixture over the asparagus. Cook as above and serve warm.

stilton & pancetta bruschetta

Serves **2**
Preparation time **5 minutes**
Cooking time **5 minutes**

1 tablespoon **olive oil**
1 **garlic clove**, crushed
100 g (4 oz) **pancetta**, cut
   into small cubes
250 g (8 oz) mixed
   mushrooms, sliced
4 tablespoons **double cream**
25 g (1 oz) **Stilton cheese**,
   crumbled
1 tablespoon chopped
   parsley
4 slices of **ciabatta**, toasted

Heat the oil in a frying pan. Add the garlic and pancetta and fry for 1–2 minutes. Stir in the mushrooms and fry for a further 2–3 minutes until cooked.

Stir in the cream and crumbled Stilton and cook for 1 minute to warm through. Add the parsley to the mixture, stir to combine and serve on 2 slices of toasted ciabatta for each person.

For Stilton & pancetta pasta, cook 300 g (10 oz) pasta in boiling water according to the instructions on the packet. Meanwhile, cook 1 crushed garlic clove, 75 g (3 oz) pancetta and 250 g (8 oz) mushrooms as above. Stir the cream and Stilton through the mushrooms and warm. Drain the pasta and mix with the cream and mushroom mixture. Garnish with chopped parsley and serve with a green salad.

summer vegetable soup

Serves **2**

Preparation time **10 minutes**

Cooking time **15 minutes**

1 teaspoon **olive oil**

½ **leek**, finely sliced

½ large **potato**, chopped

200 g (7 oz) **mixed summer vegetables**, such as peas, asparagus, broad beans and courgettes

1 tablespoon chopped **mint**

450 ml (¾ pint) **vegetable stock** (see right for homemade)

1 tablespoon **crème fraîche**

salt (optional) and **black pepper**

Heat the oil in a medium saucepan, add the leek and potato and fry for 2–3 minutes until softened.

Add the vegetables to the pan with the mint and the stock and bring to the boil. Reduce the heat and simmer for 10 minutes.

Transfer the soup to a food processor or blender and process until smooth. Return to the pan with the crème fraîche and season with salt (if liked) and pepper. Heat through and serve.

For homemade vegetable stock, heat 1 tablespoon olive oil in a large saucepan. Add 1 chopped onion, 1 chopped carrot, 4 chopped celery sticks and any available vegetable trimmings (such as celery stalks, onion skins and tomato skins) and fry for 2–3 minutes. Add 1 bouquet garni and season well with salt and pepper. Add 1.7 litres (2¾ pints) water and bring to the boil. Reduce the heat and simmer gently for 1½ hours. Strain. This makes about 1.2 litres (2 pints) of stock.

roasted peppers with haloumi

Serves **2**

Preparation time **10 minutes**
Cooking time **25 minutes**

8 **anchovy fillets**, halved
1 **garlic clove**, sliced
225 g (8 oz) **cherry tomatoes**, halved
1 tablespoon **pesto** (see pages 12–13 for homemade)
1 **red pepper**, halved, cored and deseeded
1 **yellow pepper**, halved, cored and deseeded
100 g (3½ oz) **haloumi cheese**, cut into 4 slices
1 tablespoon **olive oil**
1 handful **rocket**
1 tablespoon toasted **pine nuts**

Mix together the anchovies, garlic, tomatoes and pesto.

Put the peppers on a baking sheet, cut sides up, and fill with the anchovy mixture. Lay a slice of haloumi over each and drizzle over the oil.

Cook in a preheated oven, 220°C (425°F), Gas Mark 7, for 20–25 minutes until the peppers are tender and the cheese is golden.

Top with the rocket, scatter over the pine nuts and serve.

For chicken, pepper & haloumi pasta, halve, core and deseed 1 red and 1 yellow pepper. Place the pepper halves on a baking sheet and grill until the skin is blackened. Put them in a bowl, cover with clingfilm and leave to cool. Remove the skin from the peppers and tear the flesh into strips. Cook 250 g (8 oz) pasta shapes in boiling water according to the instructions on the packet. Drain. Mix together the peppers, anchovies, garlic, tomatoes and pesto and mix through the pasta. Scatter over 100 g (3½ oz) torn haloumi and serve with rocket and toasted pine nuts.

spinach & butter bean frittata

Serves **2**
Preparation time **10 minutes**
Cooking time **10 minutes**

1 teaspoon **olive oil**
1 **onion**, sliced
400 g (13 oz) can **butter
  beans**, rinsed and drained
200 g (7 oz) **baby spinach
  leaves**
4 **eggs**, beaten
50 g (2 oz) **ricotta cheese**
salt (optional) and **black
  pepper**

Heat the oil in a medium frying pan. Add the onion and fry for 3–4 minutes until softened. Add the beans and spinach and heat gently for 2–3 minutes until the spinach has wilted.

Pour over the eggs, then spoon over the ricotta and season with salt (if liked) and pepper. Cook until almost set, then place under a preheated hot grill and cook for 1–2 minutes until golden and set. Serve with a tomato and red onion salad.

For Stilton & broccoli frittata, heat 1 teaspoon olive oil in a frying pan and fry 1 sliced onion until softened. Add 100 g (3½ oz) small, cooked broccoli florets and fry for 2 more minutes. Add the beaten eggs and scatter through 75 g (3 oz) crumbled Stilton cheese. Cook as above until almost set then transfer to a hot grill and cook until golden.

crispy chicken with salsa verde

Serves **2**

Preparation time **10 minutes**, plus marinating

Cooking time **10 minutes**

2 boneless **chicken breasts**, skin on
1 teaspoon **olive oil**
1 **garlic clove**, crushed
1 tablespoon **soy sauce**

Salsa verde

1 handful **fresh mixed herbs** (such as parsley, thyme and basil)
1 **garlic clove**, roughly chopped
2 **cornichons**
1 tablespoon drained **capers**
1 **anchovy**
2 tablespoons **olive oil**
1 teaspoon **white wine vinegar**

Make 3 slashes across the skin side of the chicken breasts and transfer to a non-metallic dish.

Mix together the oil, garlic and soy sauce, pour the mixture over the chicken and leave to marinate for 10 minutes.

Meanwhile, make the salsa verde. Mix all the ingredients together in a blender or food processor until they form a chunky paste. Chill until required.

Heat a griddle pan or heavy-based frying pan, add the marinated chicken breasts, skin side down, and fry for 2–3 minutes. Turn and cook for a further 3–4 minutes until they are cooked through.

Serve the chicken with a spoonful of salsa verde and some potatoes.

For Greek salad, to serve as an accompaniment, toss together 250g (8 oz) halved cherry tomatoes, ¼ chopped cucumber, 1 small sliced red onion and 100 g (4 oz) crumbled feta cheese. Drizzle over 1 tablespoon of olive oil and 1 teaspoon red wine vinegar and scatter over 1 tablespoon chopped fresh oregano. Season with salt and pepper to taste.

Italian bean & artichoke salad

Serves **2**

Preparation time **10 minutes**

400 g (13 oz) can **artichoke hearts**
1 small **red onion**, sliced
100 g (3 oz) ball **mozzarella cheese**, cubed
400 g (13 oz) can **cannellini beans**, drained and rinsed
75 g (3 oz) **rocket**

Dressing

1 **red chilli**, finely chopped
1 teaspoon **cider vinegar**
1 teaspoon **Dijon mustard**
1 teaspoon **caster sugar**
1 tablespoon **olive oil**
1 tablespoon chopped **fresh mixed herbs** (such as parsley, coriander and basil)

Make the dressing. Whisk together the vinegar, mustard, sugar, oil and chopped herbs in a small bowl. Set aside.

Drain the artichoke hearts and mix them with the onion, mozzarella and beans. Add the rocket and combine.

Stir the dressing through the salad and serve.

For quick bean & feta salad, cut 2 thick slices of bread into cubes. Brush them with 1 tablespoon olive oil, transfer to a roasting tin and cook in a preheated oven, 200°C (400°F), Gas Mark 6, for 10–15 minutes until golden. Combine 200 g (7 oz) can mixed bean salad with 50 g (2 oz) chopped feta cheese. Serve with chopped cos lettuce and a handful of croutons.

chicory, mackerel & orange salad

Serves **2**
Preparation time **10 minutes**

2 heads of **chicory**
2 **mackerel** fillets, flaked
2 **oranges**, segmented
handful of **watercress**

Dressing
juice of **1 orange**
1 tablespoon **olive oil**
1 teaspoon **wholegrain
  mustard**
1 teaspoon **clear honey**

Separate the chicory into individual leaves and mix them in a large bowl with the mackerel, orange segments and watercress.

Make the dressing. Whisk together the orange juice, oil, mustard and honey.

Drizzle the dressing over the salad and serve with crusty bread.

For Gruyère & mixed seed salad, combine the leaves of 2 heads of chicory with 75 g (3 oz) chopped Gruyère cheese and about 25 g (1 oz) toasted mixed seeds and the orange and watercress as above. Drizzle over the dressing and serve.

chèvre & asparagus panini

Serves **2**
Preparation time **5 minutes**
Cooking time **18–20 minutes**

150 g (5 oz) trimmed
  asparagus spears
2 tablespoons **olive oil**
125 g (4 oz) **soft mild goats'
  cheese**
4 slices of French-style **walnut
  bread**
75 g (3 oz) **firm goats'
  cheese** with rind, sliced
1 teaspoon chopped **lemon
  thyme**
salt and **black pepper**

To serve
large handful of **rocket leaves**
2 teaspoons **truffle oil**

Toss the asparagus spears in the oil, season well and
transfer to a roasting tin. Cook in a preheated oven,
180°C (350°F), Gas Mark 4, for about 15 minutes or
until golden.

Spread the soft goats' cheese over 2 slices of walnut
bread. Top with the roasted asparagus spears and
arrange the sliced firm goats' cheese over them.

Scatter over the lemon thyme, top with the remaining
slices of bread and toast in a sandwich grill for
3–4 minutes or according to the manufacturer's
instructions until the bread is golden and the cheese
has melted. Serve with a drizzle of truffle oil.

For cheese, bacon & maple syrup panini, spread
50 g (2 oz) cream cheese over 2 slices of walnut
bread. Top each with 2 slices of grilled streaky bacon
and drizzle over 1 teaspoon maple syrup. Top each
with another slice of walnut bread and cook in a
sandwich grill as above.

pear & gorgonzola pizzas

Makes **2**
Preparation time **10 minutes**,
   plus proving
Cooking time **20 minutes**

Pizza base

1 x 7 g sachet **easy-blend
   yeast**
1 tablespoon **skimmed milk
   powder**
½ teaspoon **salt**
325 g (11 oz) **strong white
   flour**
1 teaspoon **caster sugar**
1 tablespoon **olive oil**
200 ml (7 fl oz) hand-hot
   water

Topping

1 teaspoon **olive oil**
175 g (6 oz) **pears** peeled,
   cored and cut into 16 slices
100 g (3½ oz) **Gorgonzola
   cheese**, roughly crumbled
handful **rocket**, to garnish

Mix together the yeast, milk powder, salt, flour and sugar in a large bowl. Stir the oil into the water and pour on to the flour mixture. Mix to form a soft dough, adding a little extra water or flour if necessary.

Knead on a lightly floured surface for 5 minutes. Transfer to a lightly oiled bowl, cover with a damp cloth and leave to prove in a warm place until the dough has doubled in size.

Divide the dough in 2 and knead each ball. Roll into a circle about 20 cm (8 inches) across and place on a baking sheet. Brush the dough with 1 teaspoon oil, then layer over the pear slices and scatter over the Gorgonzola cheese.

Cook in a preheated oven, 220°C (425°F), Gas Mark 7, for 15–20 minutes until golden and bubbling and the dough is browned. Serve immediately with a green salad, if liked.

For Gorgonzola, Parma ham & rocket pizzas, prepare the pizza bases as above. Heat 1 tablespoon olive oil in a frying pan and cook 1 sliced onion until softened. Arrange on the pizza bases, scatter over the Gorgonzola and cook as above. Tear 6 slices of Parma ham into pieces and lay them over the pizzas, top with a handful of rocket and a drizzle of olive oil and serve.

quick suppers

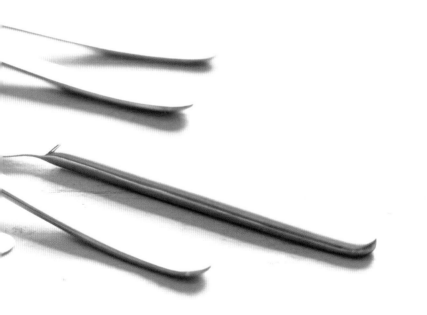

tomato, olive & feta tartlets

Serves **2**

Preparation time **10 minutes**

Cooking time **15 minutes**

175 g (6 oz) **puff pastry**,
   thawed if frozen

125 g (4 oz) **cherry
   tomatoes**, halved

12 pitted **olives**, halved

75 g (3 oz) **feta cheese**,
   crumbled

2 teaspoons **olive oil**

Pesto

large handful of **basil** leaves

1 tablespoon toasted **pine
   nuts**

1 tablespoon grated
   Parmesan cheese

1 small **garlic clove**, chopped

2 tablespoons **olive oil**

salt and **black pepper**

Divide the pastry in 2 and roll each piece into a square about 15 x 15 cm (6 x 6 inches). With a knife, lightly mark a border around each pastry square about 1 cm (½ inch) in from the edge and transfer to a baking sheet.

Make the pesto. Put the basil, pine nuts, Parmesan, garlic and oil in a blender or food processor. Season to taste with salt and process until combined but still retaining some texture. (Any leftover pesto can be stored in the refrigerator for a couple of days.)

Mix together the tomatoes, olives, feta and oil, season well and spread over the pastry squares, keeping within the border.

Drizzle 2 teaspoons pesto over the tartlets and bake in a preheated oven, 220°C (425°F), Gas Mark 7, for about 15 minutes until golden and puffed up. Serve with a crisp green salad, if liked.

For pepper & brie tartlets, prepare the pastry squares as above. Spread 1 teaspoon pesto over each, then place 1 roasted skinned and sliced red pepper within the border and top each with 2 slices of brie. Scatter over a little fresh chopped oregano and a drizzle of olive oil and cook as above.

ricotta & parma ham pasta

Serves **2**

Preparation time **10 minutes**
Cooking time **15 minutes**

175 g (6 oz) **pasta shapes**
1 tablespoon **olive oil**
1 small **onion**, finely chopped
1 **garlic clove**, crushed
75 g (3 oz) **Parma ham**, torn
   into bite-sized pieces
125 g (4 oz) **ricotta cheese**
75 g (3 oz) **rocket**
2 tablespoons grated
   Parmesan cheese
2 tablespoons **white wine**
salt and **black pepper**

Cook the pasta in boiling water according to the instructions on the packet. Drain.

Meanwhile, heat the oil in a nonstick frying pan, add the onion and garlic and fry for 3 minutes until softened. Then add the ham and cook for 1 minute.

Add the ricotta, rocket, Parmesan and wine to the pan and heat through for 1 minute. Toss the sauce through the cooked pasta, season to taste with salt and pepper and serve hot.

For ricotta, Parma ham & artichoke pasta bake,
cook 175 g (6 oz) pasta. Cook the onion and garlic as above. Add 125 g (4 oz) ricotta to the frying pan with 125 g (4 oz) drained artichoke hearts, 75 g (3 oz) Parma ham and 2 tablespoons grated Parmesan. Stir 4 tablespoons double cream through the pasta, mix in the contents of the frying pan, then pour it all into an ovenproof dish. Mix together 125 g (4 oz) chopped mozzarella and 50 g (2 oz) ciabatta breadcrumbs. Sprinkle the breadcrumb mixture over the pasta and bake in a preheated oven, 180°C (350°F), Gas Mark 4, for 10–15 minutes until golden and bubbling.

vegetable stir-fry

Serves **2**
Preparation time **10 minutes**
Cooking time **20 minutes**

1 tablespoon **olive oil** or
   rapeseed oil
½ **onion**, diced
½ **red pepper**, cored,
   deseeded and diced
1 **celery stick**, sliced
1 tablespoon **light soy sauce**
1 tablespoon **tomato ketchup**
pinch of **chilli powder**
50 g (2 oz) **mushrooms**,
   trimmed and sliced
5 **cherry tomatoes**, halved
50 g (2 oz) **mangetout** or
   French beans, halved
   if large
50 g (2 oz) **bean sprouts**
1 large **carrot**, cut into batons
spring onion curls, to garnish
   (optional)

Heat the oil in a large nonstick pan or wok. Add the onion and cook for 2 minutes.

Add the red pepper and celery and sauté for a few minutes. Add the soy sauce, tomato ketchup and chilli powder and stir well.

Add the remaining vegetables and stir-fry over a medium heat for 10–15 minutes until the vegetables are tender. Add a small amount of water if necessary.

Garnish the stir-fry with spring onion curls (if liked) and serve with wholemeal pitta bread.

For chicken & noodle stir-fry, thinly slice 2 small boneless, skinless chicken breasts and fry them with a large diced onion. Continue as above and add 100 g (3½ oz) cooked noodles once the vegetables are almost tender. Sprinkle over 2 tablespoons chopped peanuts and serve.

feta, fresh herb & rocket frittata

Serves **2**
Preparation time **5 minutes**
Cooking time **10 minutes**

4 **eggs**, beaten
2 tablespoons chopped
  herbs, such as chives,
  chervil and parsley
1 tablespoon **double cream**
1 tablespoon **olive oil**
1 small **red onion**, finely sliced
½ **red pepper**, deseeded and
  finely sliced
100 g (3½ oz) **feta cheese**
large handful of **rocket leaves**
salt and **black pepper**

Beat together the eggs, herbs and cream.

Heat the oil in a nonstick frying pan with an ovenproof handle, add the onion and pepper and fry for 3–4 minutes until just softened. Pour in the egg mixture and cook for about 3 minutes until almost set.

Crumble over the feta, then cook under a preheated hot grill until golden. Top with the rocket and serve.

For potato & goats' cheese frittata, beat together the eggs, herbs and cream as above. Add 150 g (5 oz) cooked and sliced new potatoes to the egg mixture and cook as above. Arrange 4 slices of firm goats' cheese over the frittata and finish cooking under a preheated hot grill. Serve with rocket.

cabbage & anchovy pasta

Serves **2**
Preparation time **5 minutes**
Cooking time **15 minutes**

175 g (6 oz) **pasta shapes**
1 tablespoon **olive oil**
¼ **Savoy cabbage**, finely
  shredded
1 **garlic clove**, sliced
4 **anchovies**, finely chopped
2 tablespoons **pine nuts**
2 tablespoons grated
  Parmesan cheese

Cook the pasta in boiling water according to the instructions on the packet. Drain and keep warm.

Meanwhile, heat the oil in a frying pan. Add the cabbage and garlic and cook for 5–6 minutes until the cabbage is tender. Add the anchovies, pine nuts and Parmesan and stir to combine.

Toss the cabbage mixture through the pasta and serve immediately.

For creamy spinach pasta, cook 175 g (6 oz) pasta as above. Heat 1 tablespoon olive oil and cook 175 g (6 oz) baby leaf spinach for 5–6 minutes. Omit the anchovies but instead add 2 tablespoons mascarpone and 1 tablespoon grated Parmesan to the pan. Stir the spinach mixture through the pasta and serve.

chicken with potatoes & beans

Serves **2**

Preparation time **10 minutes**, plus marinating

Cooking time **15 minutes**

2 boneless, skinless **chicken breasts**

1 tablespoon **pesto** (see pages 12–13 for homemade)

2 tablespoons **mascarpone cheese**

Potatoes

250 g (8 oz) new **potatoes**

2 tablespoons **crème fraîche**

1 tablespoon **wholegrain mustard**

4 **spring onions**, chopped

Green beans

150 g (5 oz) **French beans**

1 teaspoon **olive oil**

15 g (½ oz) **butter**

1 **garlic clove**, crushed

Make 3 deep slashes in the top of each chicken breast and place them in a non-metallic dish. Mix together the pesto and mascarpone, pour over the chicken and leave to marinate for 10 minutes.

Heat a griddle pan or frying pan until hot and cook the chicken breasts for 3–4 minutes on each side until cooked through. Pour over any remaining marinade and heat through for 1 minute.

Meanwhile, cook the potatoes in boiling salted water until tender. Drain and toss through the crème fraîche, mustard and spring onions, and gently crush with the back of a fork.

Cook the beans in a small saucepan of boiling water for 2 minutes and drain. Heat the oil and butter in a frying pan, add the garlic and fry for 1 minute, add the beans and stir-fry for 1 minute. Serve the chicken with the potatoes and beans.

For creamy pesto chicken tortillas, prepare a marinade of 1 tablespoon pesto and 2 tablespoons mascarpone cheese. Marinate the chicken in the mixture for at least 10 minutes, then cook as above. Allow to cool slightly and cut into 1 cm (½ inch) slices. Roll the chicken slices in warmed flour tortillas, spoon over any remaining marinade and serve with plenty of fresh green salad.

open chicken & spinach ravioli

Serves **2**
Preparation time **5 minutes**
Cooking time **10 minutes**

1 tablespoon **olive oil**
1 large **chicken breast**, thinly
    sliced
1 **garlic clove**, crushed
200 g (7 oz) **baby leaf**
    spinach
150 g (5 oz) **ricotta cheese**
good pinch of **grated nutmeg**
1 tablespoon grated
    Parmesan cheese, plus
    extra to serve
3 fresh **pasta sheets**, halved
salt and **black pepper**

Heat half the oil in a nonstick frying pan, add the
chicken and fry for 2–3 minutes or until just cooked.
Add the garlic and spinach and cook until the spinach
is wilted and any excess liquid has evaporated.

Add the ricotta, nutmeg and Parmesan to the pan, stir
through and remove from the heat. Season to taste
with salt and pepper.

Meanwhile, cook the pasta in boiling water for about
5 minutes or until just cooked. Drain. On each serving
plate layer 3 pieces of pasta with the chicken mixture,
finishing with a piece of pasta on top. Sprinkle with
Parmesan, drizzle over the remaining oil and serve.

For open vegetarian ravioli, arrange a good
selection of vegetables (such as cored, deseeded
and sliced peppers, sliced courgettes, mushrooms,
sliced aubergine and chopped onion) on a baking
sheet. Drizzle with olive oil and scatter over a handful
of fresh herbs. Cook in a preheated oven, 180°C
(350°F), Gas Mark 4, for 15–20 minutes. Layer the
vegetables onto the cooked pasta sheets with 75 g
(3 oz) torn mozzarella. Top with the pasta sheets as
above and sprinkle over some grated Parmesan
before serving.

citrus chicken with rice salad

Serves **2**

Preparation time **10 minutes**, plus marinating

Cooking time **15 minutes**

2 boneless, skinless **chicken breasts**, sliced lengthways into strips

2 tablespoons **buttermilk**

grated rind and juice of ½ **lime**

1 **garlic clove**, crushed

pinch of **ground coriander**

1 tablespoon chopped **fresh coriander**

Rice salad

100 g (3½ oz) **mixed basmati** and **wild rice**

1 tablespoon **olive oil**

4 **spring onions**, sliced

25 g (1 oz) **cashew nuts**, roughly chopped

handful of **baby leaf spinach**

grated rind and juice of 1 **orange**

1 tablespoon **soy sauce**

Put the chicken strips in a non-metallic dish. Mix together the buttermilk, lime rind and juice and garlic, pour the mixture over the chicken, turn to coat evenly and set aside for at least 10 minutes. Alternatively, prepare the marinade in the morning and leave the chicken in it in the refrigerator all day.

Cook the rice according to the instructions on the packet. Drain thoroughly.

Heat the oil in a small frying pan. Fry the spring onions for 1 minute. Toss the onions through the rice, and then add the cashew nuts, spinach, orange rind and juice and soy sauce. Set aside.

Thread the chicken evenly on 4 skewers and cook, turning from time to time, under a preheated hot grill for 4–5 minutes. Serve with the rice salad.

For monkfish & prawn skewers, instead of the chicken, prepare a marinade with 2 tablespoons buttermilk, the grated rind and juice of ½ lime, a crushed garlic clove and a pinch of coriander. Marinade 200 g (7 oz) firm white monkfish, cut into cubes, and 12 raw tiger prawns for at least 20 minutes. Prepare the rice salad as above, before threading the fish and prawns on to 4 presoaked bamboo skewers and cook, turning, under a preheated hot grill until the fish is cooked through.

chicken ratatouille

Serves **2**

Preparation time **20 minutes**

Cooking time **20–25 minutes**

2 tablespoons **olive oil**

2 boneless, skinless **chicken breasts**, each about 150 g (5 oz), cut into 2.5 cm (1 inch) pieces

60 g (2¼ oz) **courgettes**, thinly sliced

75 g (3 oz) **aubergine**, cubed

150 g (5 oz) **onion**, thinly sliced

50 g (2 oz) **green pepper**, deseeded and sliced

75 g (3 oz) **mushrooms**, sliced

400 g (13 oz) can **chopped tomatoes**

2 **garlic cloves**, finely chopped

1 teaspoon **vegetable stock powder**

1 teaspoon crushed dried **basil**

1 teaspoon dried **parsley**

½ teaspoon **black pepper**

fresh basil leaves, to garnish

Heat the oil in a large frying pan. Add the chicken and cook, stirring, for about 2 minutes. Add the courgettes, aubergine, onion, green pepper and mushrooms. Cook, stirring occasionally, for about 15 minutes, or until tender.

Add the tomatoes to the pan, stirring gently. Stir in the garlic, vegetable stock powder, basil, parsley and pepper and simmer, uncovered, for about 5 minutes or until a fork goes easily into the chicken.

Serve garnished with the fresh basil leaves.

For stuffed ratatouille peppers, make the ratatouille as above but omit the chicken. Halve, core and deseed 2 red peppers and place them in an ovenproof dish. Spoon the ratatouille into the pepper halves and sprinkle over 100 g (3½ oz) chopped mozzarella cheese. Cook in a preheated oven, 180°C (350°F), Gas Mark 4, for 20 minutes or until the peppers are tender.

shish kebabs & tzatziki pittas

Serves **2**
Preparation time **10 minutes**
Cooking time **5 minutes**

250 g (8 oz) **lamb mince**
½ teaspoon **ground cumin**
½ teaspoon **ground coriander**
2 tablespoons roughly chopped **fresh coriander**
1 **garlic clove**, halved
½ small **onion**, roughly chopped

Tzatziki
4 tablespoons **Greek yogurt**
1 **garlic clove**, crushed
¼ **cucumber**, finely chopped
1 tablespoon chopped **parsley**

Make the tzatziki. Mix together the yogurt, crushed garlic, cucumber and chopped parsley, transfer to a small bowl and set aside.

Put the lamb, cumin, ground and fresh coriander, garlic and onion in a food processor and blend until well combined but still retaining a little texture.

Divide the mixture into 4 and use damp hands to shape it around 4 metal or presoaked bamboo skewers. Cook under a preheated hot grill for 3–4 minutes, turning regularly until browned and the lamb is just cooked through.

Serve 2 kebabs in a toasted pitta bread with crisp green salad and a spoonful of tzatziki.

For pork burgers & tzatziki rolls, combine in a food processor 250 g (8 oz) pork mince with ½ teaspoon each ground cumin and ground coriander, 2 tablespoons chopped fresh coriander, a garlic clove and ½ small onion. Process briefly so that the mixture retains some texture. Divide the mixture in half and shape it into 2 burgers. Cook the burgers on a preheated hot griddle for 2–3 minutes on each side and serve in a toasted roll with salad and a spoonful of tzatziki.

smoked haddock fishcakes

Serves **2**
Preparation time **10 minutes**,
  plus chilling
Cooking time **40 minutes**

200 g (7 oz) **smoked
  haddock**, skinned
200 ml (7 fl oz) **milk**
2 **spring onions**, sliced
1 tablespoon **mayonnaise**
1 tablespoon chopped **dill**,
  plus extra sprigs to garnish
500 g (1 lb) cooked **potato**,
  mashed
vegetable oil, for frying

To coat
1 tablespoon **seasoned flour**
1 **egg**, beaten
100 g (3½ oz) fresh
  breadcrumbs

Potato wedges
2 large **potatoes**, cut into
  wedges and parboiled
1 tablespoon **olive oil**
3 **garlic cloves** with skin on
salt and **black pepper**

Put the fish in a saucepan, pour over the milk and simmer for 5 minutes. Discard the milk and flake the fish from the skin. Mix together in a bowl the flaked fish with the spring onions, mayonnaise, dill and mashed potato.

Shape the mixture into 4 patties. Dip each fishcake in the seasoned flour, then in egg and finally in breadcrumbs, ensuring that they are all evenly coated. Chill for least 30 minutes.

Put the parboiled potato wedges in a baking tin with the oil and garlic. Season with salt and pepper. Cook in a preheated oven, 200°C (400°F), Gas Mark 6, for 30–40 minutes until golden.

Heat a little oil in a frying pan and fry the fishcakes for 1–2 minutes on each side until golden. Serve garnished with the sprigs of dill, with the potato wedges and a good squeeze of lemon.

For crab cakes, heat 1 tablespoon olive oil in a frying pan. Fry ½ chopped onion and 1 finely chopped green pepper for 3–4 minutes and add 1 crushed garlic clove and 2–3 finely chopped spring onions. Fry a further 3–4 minutes and tip into a bowl. Mix 50 g (2 oz) breadcrumbs with 125 g (4 oz) white and brown crabmeat, 1 tablespoon Worcestershire sauce, a good pinch of cayenne pepper, 1–2 tablespoons chopped parsley and a lightly beaten egg. Season with salt. Mix with the onion mixture and shape into 2 balls. Flatten them between your hands to make 2 cakes. Heat a little sunflower oil in a frying pan and fry the cakes for 4–5 minutes on each side.

parmesan & polenta plaice

Serves **2**
Preparation time **10 minutes**
Cooking time **10 minutes**

2 skinned **plaice fillets**
1 **egg**, beaten
2 tablespoons **polenta**
2 tablespoons grated
  Parmesan cheese
pinch of **cayenne pepper**
vegetable oil, for frying

Tartare sauce
1 tablespoon **mayonnaise**
1 tablespoon **crème fraîche**
1 **gherkin**, finely chopped
1 tablespoon **capers**, rinsed
  and roughly chopped
1 teaspoon chopped **dill**
grated rind and juice of
  ½ **lime**

Make the tartare sauce. In a small bowl mix together the mayonnaise, crème fraîche, gherkin, capers, dill and lime rind and juice.

Cut the plaice into strips and dip each strip in the beaten egg. Mix together the polenta, Parmesan and cayenne, and coat the fish strips evenly in the mixture.

Heat a little oil in a frying pan. Add the plaice strips, in batches if necessary, and fry for 2–3 minutes, turning occasionally to prevent burning.

Serve the goujons in a soft roll with salad and a spoonful of tartare sauce.

For Parmesan-crusted chicken with sweet potato chips, peel 2 large sweet potatoes and cut the flesh into thick chips. Toss the chips in 1 tablespoon olive oil, sprinkle over a pinch of cayenne pepper and a little salt and roast in a preheated oven, 200°C (400°F), Gas Mark 6, for 30 minutes, then toss together with a handful of fresh chopped herbs. Cut 2 skinless chicken fillets into strips and coat them in beaten egg and the polenta, Parmesan and cayenne mix. Heat some vegetable oil in a frying pan and cook the chicken strips for 4–5 minutes. Serve the chicken with the sweet potato chips and a green salad.

rocket pesto mussels in parcels

Serves **2**

Preparation time **20 minutes**, plus preparing the mussels

Cooking time **15–20 minutes**

1 kg (2 lb) **mussels**, scrubbed and debearded

2 tablespoons **rocket pesto** (see below for homemade)

Lemon breadcrumbs

about 40 g (1½ oz) small, stale **baguette** or other crusty bread

finely grated rind of ½ **lemon**

1 **garlic clove**, finely chopped

1 tablespoon **olive oil**

1 tablespoon chopped **flat-leaf parsley**

¼ teaspoon crushed **dried red chillies** (optional)

Prepare the breadcrumbs. Put the bread in a clean, dry food processor and process into crumbs. Add the lemon rind, garlic, oil, parsley and chillies (if using) and mix well.

Heat a nonstick frying pan over a low heat and add the breadcrumb mixture. Toast gently for about 5 minutes, stirring frequently to prevent burning, until crisp and golden. Transfer the breadcrumbs to a plate lined with paper towels to absorb any excess oil and leave to cool.

Mix the dry mussels with the pesto sauce in a dry bowl until thoroughly coated, then divide between 2 large pieces of foil. Fold up the edges and scrunch them together to seal. Heat a griddle pan over a medium heat, put the foil parcels directly on the griddle and cook for 15–20 minutes until the mussels have opened. Discard any that remain closed.

Put the foil parcels in warm bowls. Diners open the parcels themselves and sprinkle the crispy breadcrumbs over the mussels and add more pesto to taste. Serve with cooked asparagus tips and plenty of crusty bread.

For homemade rocket pesto, to mix with the mussels, put 300 g (10 oz) roughly chopped rocket, 1 small finely chopped garlic clove, 75 ml (3 fl oz) olive oil and 1½ tablespoons lightly toasted pine nuts in a food processor or blender and process until fairly smooth. Pour into a bowl and stir in 1 tablespoon grated Parmesan cheese, 1 tablespoon lemon juice and 50 ml (2 fl oz) soured cream. Season to taste with salt and pepper. These quantities make 300 ml (½ pint).

sweet potato & roquefort toasts

Serves **2**
Preparation time **5 minutes**
Cooking time **12 minutes**

50 ml (2 fl oz) **clear honey**
1 teaspoon crushed **red
  pepper flakes**
50 ml (2 fl oz) **sesame oil**
100 ml (3½ fl oz) **olive oil**
1 large **sweet potato**, peeled
  and thickly sliced
50 g (2 oz) **sugar snap peas**
2 ready-made **potato cakes**
  (see below for homemade)
  or **pitta breads**
50 g (2 oz) **Roquefort**
salt and **black pepper**

Mix together the honey, red pepper flakes, sesame oil and olive oil in a small bowl. Put the sweet potato slices and sugar snap peas in a large bowl and toss them with half of the honey dressing until they are evenly coated. Season to taste with salt and pepper.

Transfer the vegetables to a baking sheet, arranging them so the potatoes are in a single layer. Cook under a preheated hot grill for 8 minutes, turning occasionally, until the potatoes are soft and turning golden.

When they are cool enough to handle, arrange the potato slices and peas over one of the potato cakes and crumble the blue cheese over the top.

Top with the remaining potato cake to create a sandwich and toast in a sandwich grill for 3–4 minutes or according to the manufacturer's instructions until the potato cake is golden and the cheese is just melting. Cut in half and serve immediately with a small bowl of the remaining honey dressing to drizzle if liked.

For homemade potato cakes, mix together 50 g (2 oz) unsalted butter with 250 g (8 oz) self-raising flour. Add 175 g (6 oz) cooked mashed potato and 3–4 tablespoons milk to make a soft dough. Roll out on a lightly floured surface to about 2.5 cm (1 inch) thickness and cut into 12 rounds with a biscuit cutter. Transfer to a lightly greased baking sheet and cook in a preheated oven, 200°C (400°F), Gas Mark 6, for 15–18 minutes.

salmon curry with tomato salad

Serves **2**
Preparation time **10 minutes**
Cooking time **20 minutes**

1 teaspoon **vegetable oil**
15 g (½ oz) **butter**
1 small **onion**, sliced
1 **garlic clove**, chopped
1 teaspoon **tandoori spice mix**
1 **cinnamon stick**
150 g (5 oz) **cherry tomatoes**, halved
4 tablespoons **crème fraîche**
grated rind and juice of ½ **lime**
200 g (7 oz) skinless **salmon fillet**, cut into chunks
1 tablespoon chopped **mint**
1 tablespoon chopped **fresh coriander**

Tomato & onion salad
150 g (5 oz) vine-ripened **tomatoes**, thinly sliced
1 small **red onion**, finely sliced
handful of **fresh coriander**, chopped
1 teaspoon **lemon juice**

Heat the oil and butter in a small frying pan. Add the onion and garlic and fry for 2–3 minutes until softened. Stir in the spice mix and cinnamon stick and fry for a further minute. Add the tomatoes, crème fraîche, lime rind and juice and heat for a minute.

Put the salmon in an ovenproof dish. Spoon over the sauce, cover the dish tightly with foil and cook in a preheated oven, 200°C (400°F), Gas Mark 6, for 15–20 minutes or until the salmon is just cooked.

Meanwhile, make the salad by tossing together the tomatoes, onion and coriander. Dress with lemon juice.

Serve the salmon with basmati rice and the tomato and onion salad.

For paneer curry, prepare the sauce as above. Cut 150 g (5 oz) paneer into cubes and put the pieces in an ovenproof dish. Pour over the sauce, making sure the paneer cubes are evenly coated, cover with foil and cook as above. Serve with boiled rice and the tomato and onion salad.

prawn balls & sweet chilli sauce

Serves **2**
Preparation time **10 minutes**
Cooking time **5 minutes**

300 g (10 oz) raw **tiger
  prawns**, shelled
2 **spring onions**, roughly
  chopped
grated rind of ½ **lime**
1 tablespoon chopped **fresh
  coriander**
1 teaspoon **fish sauce**
  (nam pla)
1 tablespoon **cornflour**
groundnut oil, for frying

Sweet chilli sauce
2 tablespoons **rice wine
  vinegar**
1 tablespoon **caster sugar**
1 **red chilli**, finely chopped
½ **red onion**, finely chopped
1 tablespoon chopped **fresh
  coriander**

Put the prawns, spring onions, lime rind, coriander and fish sauce in a food processor or blender and process for about 20 seconds until well combined but retaining a little texture.

Shape the mixture into 12 balls and lightly dust them in cornflour. Heat a little oil in a nonstick frying pan and fry the balls for 2–3 minutes until golden all over. Drain on kitchen paper.

Meanwhile, make the chilli sauce. Put the vinegar and sugar in a small saucepan and heat gently to dissolve the sugar. Increase the heat and boil for a couple of minutes until the mixture becomes syrupy. Add the chilli and red onion and allow to cool, then stir through the coriander.

Serve the prawn balls with the chilli sauce in a bowl for dipping, and a crisp green salad, if liked.

For cod balls & sweet chilli sauce, combine 300 g (10 oz) skinless cod fillet (or any other firm white fish) with the spring onions, lime rind, chopped fresh coriander and fish sauce as above. Make 12 balls and roll them to coat lightly in cornflour. Fry in vegetable oil and serve with the chilli sauce, made as above, and steamed rice or warm pitta bread.

hot haloumi with fattoush salad

Serves **2**
Preparation time **10 minutes**
Cooking time **2–4 minutes**

2 teaspoons **olive oil**
250 g (8 oz) **haloumi cheese**,
  thickly sliced

Fattoush salad
75 g (3 oz) **red pepper**, finely
  sliced
75 g (3 oz) **yellow pepper**,
  finely sliced
75 g (3 oz) **cucumber**,
  chopped
75 g (3 oz) **spring onions**,
  finely chopped
2 tablespoons chopped **flat-
  leaf parsley**
2 tablespoons chopped **mint**
2 tablespoons chopped **fresh
  coriander**

Dressing
1 teaspoon crushed **garlic**
2 tablespoons **olive oil** or
  flaxseed oil
4 tablespoons **lemon juice**
salt and **black pepper**

Heat the oil in a nonstick frying pan. Add the haloumi and fry over a medium to high heat for 1–2 minutes on each side until golden brown. Keep warm.

Make the salad. Put the red and yellow peppers, cucumber, spring onions, parsley, mint and coriander in a bowl and stir to combine.

Make the dressing. Mix the garlic with the oil and lemon juice and season to taste with salt and pepper.

Pour the dressing over the salad and toss lightly to mix. Serve with the warm haloumi.

For chicken fattoush salad, replace the haloumi with 2 boneless, skinless chicken breasts, cut in half horizontally. Heat 1 teaspoon olive oil in a frying pan and cook the chicken for 2 minutes on each side until cooked through. Keep warm while you prepare the salad and dressing. Serve the warm chicken on top of the salad.

haddock, braised lettuce & peas

Serves **2**
Preparation time **5 minutes**
Cooking time **10 minutes**

1 tablespoon **olive oil**
2 **haddock loins**, skinned
1 **Little Gem lettuce**,
  quartered
100 ml (3½ fl oz) **fish stock**
200 g (7 oz) **frozen peas**
1 tablespoon chopped **mint**
4 tablespoons **crème fraîche**

Heat the oil in a nonstick frying pan. Add the fish and cook for a minute on each side, then add the lettuce, stock and peas. Cover and simmer for 4 minutes.

Remove the lid and stir through the mint and crème fraîche. Heat through again and serve with steamed new potatoes, if liked.

For fried chicken with braised lettuce & peas,

first make homemade chicken stock. Put 1 large chicken carcass, plus any trimmings and the giblets, except the liver, if available, 1 quartered onion, 1 roughly chopped celery stick, 1 bouquet garni or 3 bay leaves and 1 teaspoon black peppercorns into a large, heavy-based saucepan and add 1.8 litres (3 pints) cold water and bring slowly to the boil. Reduce the heat and simmer gently for 1½ hours, skimming the surface from time to time if necessary. Strain the stock through a large sieve but don't squeeze the juice out of the vegetables or the stock will be cloudy. Leave the stock to cool completely, then chill. Remove any layer of fat that sets on the surface before use. These ingredients will make about 1 litre (1¾ pints). Meanwhile, cook 2 boneless, skinless chicken breasts, each about 150 g (5 oz), in 1 tablespoon olive oil in a nonstick frying pan. Add the lettuce and peas as above and 100 ml (3½ fl oz) chicken stock. Stir in the mint and crème fraîche, heat gently and serve.

sausage & broccoli pasta

Serves **2**

Preparation time **5 minutes**

Cooking time **10–15 minutes**

175 g (6 oz) **pasta shapes**

250 g (8 oz) **broccoli**, cut into florets

1 tablespoon **olive oil**

4 good-quality **pork sausages**

pinch of **chilli flakes**

6 tablespoons **vegetable stock** (see page 94 for homemade)

2 tablespoons grated **Parmesan cheese**

Cook the pasta in boiling water according to the instructions on the packet, adding the broccoli about 3 minutes before the end of the cooking time.

Meanwhile, heat the oil in a frying pan. Add the sausages and fry for 4–5 minutes over a medium heat until browned all over. Remove from the pan and cut each into 4 or 5 pieces. Return to the pan, add the chilli flakes and stock and cook for a further 2 minutes.

Drain the pasta and broccoli and toss together with the sausage mix. Serve sprinkled with the Parmesan and place under a preheated grill for 2–3 minutes, if liked.

For Mediterranean sausage & broccoli pasta, cook the pasta as above, adding the broccoli florets 3 minutes before the end of the cooking time. Fry 150 g (5 oz) sliced chorizo for about 5 minutes in 1 tablespoon olive oil, then add 6 tablespoons beef or chicken stock and the chilli flakes. Just before serving toss through 100 g (3½ oz) halved cherry tomatoes.

sausage, chorizo & bean stew

Serves **2**
Preparation time **10 minutes**
Cooking time **25 minutes**

1 tablespoon **olive oil**
75 g (3 oz) **chorizo**, chopped
1 small **onion**, sliced
1 **garlic clove**, sliced
½ teaspoon **paprika**
4 good-quality **pork
sausages**, sliced
200 g (7 oz) **cherry tomatoes**
200 ml (7 fl oz) **beef stock**
400 g (13 oz) can **cannellini
beans**, rinsed and drained
1 tablespoon chopped
parsley, to garnish

Garlic ciabatta

2 small, individual **ciabatta
loaves**
40 g (1½ oz) **butter**, softened
1 **garlic clove**, crushed
1 tablespoon chopped **herbs**,
such as parsley, chives and
thyme
½ small **red chilli**, finely
chopped

Heat the oil in a large pan. Add the chorizo, onion, garlic and paprika and fry for 2 minutes until the onion begins to soften. Remove from the pan and set aside.

Add the sausages to the pan and fry for 2–3 minutes until browned all over. Return the onion mixture to the pan along with the tomatoes, stock and beans. Bring to the boil, cover and transfer to a preheated oven, 180°C (350°F), Gas Mark 4, and cook for 20 minutes.

Meanwhile, make 5 deep cuts in each ciabatta loaf. Mix together the butter, garlic and herbs and spread into the cuts. Wrap the bread in foil and put them in the oven for 10–15 minutes before the end of the cooking time.

Scatter the parsley over the stew and serve with the garlic ciabatta.

For bean & potato stew, omit the chorizo and fry the onion, garlic and paprika as above. Add the tomatoes, 200 ml (7 fl oz) vegetable stock (see page 94 for homemade) and cannellini beans to the pan with 250 g (8 oz) cooked and halved new potatoes and 125 g (4 oz) halved green beans. Cook in the oven as above and serve garnished with chopped parsley.

baby leek & serrano ham gratin

Serves **2**
Preparation time **10 minutes**
Cooking time **20 minutes**

12 baby **leeks**, trimmed and
  cleaned
6 slices of **Serrano ham**
15 g (½ oz) **butter**
15 g (½ oz) **plain flour**
300 ml (½ pint) **full-fat milk**
50 g (2 oz) granary
  breadcrumbs
50 g (2 oz) **Gruyère cheese**
8 **cherry tomatoes**, halved
  (optional)

Steam the leeks for 2–3 minutes or until tender.
Cut the ham slices in half and wrap each leek in
half a piece ham. Place the leeks in the bottom of an
ovenproof dish that is just large enough to hold them.

Melt the butter in a small saucepan. Add the flour
and cook for 1 minute, stirring. Gradually add the milk,
stirring continuously, until you have a smooth sauce.
Simmer for 1 minute then pour over the leeks.

Mix together the breadcrumbs and cheese and sprinkle
over the leeks. Arrange the tomatoes (if using) on top,
cut side up. Cook in a preheated oven, 200°C (400°F),
Gas Mark 6, for 20 minutes until golden and bubbling.

For broccoli gratin, steam 100 g (3½ oz) broccoli
florets. Arrange them in the base of a small ovenproof
dish. Make the sauce as above and pour it over the
broccoli. Mix 50 g (2 oz) fresh breadcrumbs with
50 g (2 oz) Cambozola or another creamy blue
cheese. Sprinkle over the top and cook as above.

beef & basil meatballs

Serves **2**
Preparation time **10 minutes**
Cooking time **20 minutes**

Meatballs
250 g (8 oz) lean **beef mince**
1 tablespoon grated
  Parmesan cheese
1 tablespoon **pesto** (see
  pages 12–13)
1 **egg yolk**
1 tablespoon fresh
  breadcrumbs
1 tablespoon **olive oil**

Sauce
1 small **red onion**, chopped
1 **garlic clove**, crushed
200 g (7 oz) can **chopped
  tomatoes**
2 tablespoons **single cream**
handful of **basil**, torn

Mix together the mince, Parmesan, pesto, egg yolk and breadcrumbs in a bowl. Roll the mixture between damp palms to make 20 balls.

Heat the oil in a frying pan. Add the meatballs and cook for 2–3 minutes until browned all over. Remove from the pan and set aside on kitchen paper to drain.

Add the onion and garlic to the pan and fry for 2–3 minutes. Add the tomatoes, bring to the boil and simmer for 5 minutes.

Add the meatballs to the pan with the cream and cook for a further 5 minutes. Stir in the torn basil leaves.

Serve the meatballs with the sauce, accompanied by pasta and green salad, if liked.

For pork & chilli meatballs, mix 250 g (8 oz) lean pork mince with the Parmesan, pesto, egg yolk and breadcrumbs as above to make 20 balls. Cook as above. Make the sauce with an onion and garlic clove, chopped tomatoes and cream, and add a finely chopped, deseeded green chilli. Cook the sauce as above. Serve the meatballs with steamed rice and a green salad, if liked.

steak with anchovy herb butter

Serves **2**

Preparation time **10 minutes**

Cooking time **10 minutes**

2 **sirloin steaks**

1 teaspoon **vegetable oil**

salt and **black pepper**

Herb butter

25 g (1 oz) **unsalted butter**, slightly softened

3 **anchovy fillets**, drained and finely chopped

1 tablespoon chopped **herbs**, such as chives, parsley and coriander

Rub the steak with the oil and season to taste with salt and pepper. Heat a frying pan or griddle until it is really hot and cook the steak for 2 minutes on each side or until cooked to your liking.

Mash together the butter, anchovy fillets and herbs. Put half the flavoured butter on each steak and serve with chicory and Roquefort salad (see below) and new potatoes, if liked.

For chicory & Roquefort salad, to serve as an accompaniment, mix together in a serving bowl 2 chicory heads, broken into individual leaves, 75 g (3 oz) crumbled Roquefort cheese and 25 g (1 oz) toasted and roughly chopped hazelnuts. Drizzle over a little olive oil.

calamari with citrus & garlic mayo

Serves **2**

Preparation time **10 minutes**

Cooking time **10 minutes**

2 tablespoons **plain flour**

large pinch of **chilli flakes**

8 **calamari** tubes, cut into
  rings

vegetable oil, for deep frying

1 tablespoon **lemon juice**

Citrus & garlic mayonnaise

1 **garlic clove**, crushed

1 **egg yolk**

100 ml (3½ fl oz) **olive oil**

finely grated rind and juice of
  ½ **lime** or **lemon**

1 tablespoon chopped **herbs**,
  such as fresh coriander and
  parsley

Make the citrus and garlic mayonnaise. Put the garlic, egg yolk and lime or lemon juice and rind in a food processor or blender, process and then gradually pour in the oil, while still blending, to give a thick mayonnaise. Stir through the herbs.

Mix together the flour and chilli flakes and coat the calamari. Heat a little oil in a frying pan. Add the calamari and fry in batches until golden. Toss with the lemon juice. Serve the calamari with spoonfuls of the mayonnaise and a green salad, if liked.

For garlic prawns with citrus & garlic mayo, mix together 1 crushed garlic clove, ½ teaspoon paprika, ½ red chilli, deseeded and finely chopped, 1 tablespoon olive oil and a little salt in a large bowl. Add 250 g (8 oz) large whole raw prawns. Heat a large, nonstick frying pan and cook the prawns, in a single layer, for 2–3 minutes. Turn and cook for a further 1–2 minutes. Transfer to a warm dish and serve with the citrus and garlic mayo (above).

special occasions

lamb burger & roasted tomatoes

Serves **2**

Preparation time **12 minutes**,
  plus chilling

Cooking time **1¼ hours**

275 g (9 oz) good-quality
  coarsely **minced lamb**
40 g (1½ oz) ready-to-eat
  dried apricots, finely
  chopped
1–2 tablespoons finely
  chopped **fresh coriander**
1 tablespoon finely chopped
  flat-leaf parsley
1 **garlic clove**, crushed
1 teaspoon **ground cumin**
large pinch of **cayenne
  pepper**
large pinch of **turmeric**
salt and **black pepper**

Roasted tomatoes

3 medium **plum tomatoes**,
  halved
large pinch of **paprika**
1 **garlic clove**, chopped
2 teaspoons **olive oil**

To serve

2 **soft rolls**
salad leaves

Arrange the tomatoes, cut side up, on a lightly greased nonstick baking sheet. Sprinkle over the paprika and chopped garlic and season well with salt and pepper. Drizzle with olive oil and roast in a preheated oven, 150°C (300°F) Gas Mark 2, for 1 hour. Remove and set aside until needed.

Mix the lamb, apricots, herbs and spices in a large bowl and season well with salt and pepper. Divide the mixture in half and form them into 2 balls. Flatten into burgers. Cover and chill for 30 minutes.

Heat a griddle pan or barbecue until very hot. Brush the burgers with a little oil and cook them for 5 minutes on each side, depending on how well done you like them.

Toast the halved rolls on a hot griddle pan or barbecue and top each base with salad leaves and a burger. Put 3 roasted tomatoes on each burger and top with the lid of the roll.

For mozzarella lamb burgers, prepare 275 g (9 oz) minced lamb as above, but when you have divided the mixture into 2, flatten each portion. Shape each around 15 g (½ oz) mozzarella cheese and 3 fresh coriander leaves. Smooth the meat into a burger shape and cook and serve as above.

prawn, pea & lemon risotto

Serves **2**
Preparation time **10 minutes**
Cooking time **20 minutes**

1 teaspoon **olive oil**
½ small **onion**, finely chopped
1 **garlic clove**, finely chopped
125 g (4 oz) **risotto rice**
1 tablespoon **white wine**
400 ml (14 fl oz) hot **fish stock**
grated rind and juice of ½ **lemon**
250 g (8 oz) cooked **king prawns**
150 g (5 oz) **frozen peas**
15 g (½ oz) **butter**
2 tablespoons grated **Parmesan cheese**
1 tablespoon chopped **parsley**
salt and **black pepper**

Heat the oil in a frying pan. Add the onion and garlic and fry for 2–3 minutes until softened. Add the rice and cook for a further minute, making sure that the rice is coated in the oil. Add the wine and cook for a further minute, and then gradually add the stock, ladle by ladle, stirring continuously and allowing each addition of stock to be absorbed before adding the next.

Add the prawns and peas with the final ladleful of stock and add the lemon rind and juice. Stir until the prawns and peas are cooked and heated through. Remove the pan from the heat and stir through the butter, Parmesan and parsley. Season to taste with salt and pepper and serve.

For broccoli & bean risotto, cook the onion, garlic and rice as above, adding 1 tablespoon white wine and 400 ml (14 fl oz) vegetable stock (see page 94 for homemade). When the stock has been absorbed add 125 g (4 oz) small broccoli florets and 40 g (1½ oz) frozen broad beans. When the broccoli and beans are cooked, after about 4–5 minutes, remove the risotto from the heat and stir through 15 g (½ oz) butter, 2 tablespoons grated Parmesan and 1 tablespoon chopped flat leaf parsley.

baked lemon sole & asparagus

Serves **2**

Preparation time **10 minutes**
Cooking time **20 minutes**

15 g (½ oz) **unsalted butter**,
   softened
1 tablespoon chopped **herbs**,
   such as parsley, thyme and
   chives
4 skinned **lemon sole fillets**
4 **spring onions**, shredded
1 **carrot**, cut into matchsticks
1 tablespoon **white wine**
finely grated rind of ½ **lemon**
salt and **black pepper**

Pan-fried asparagus
15 g (½ oz) **unsalted butter**
1–2 teaspoons **olive oil**
125 g (4 oz) **asparagus**
   spears
Parmesan cheese shavings

Mix together the butter and herbs and spread on to one side of each of the sole fillets. Roll up the fish with the herb butter on the inside.

Cut 4 squares of baking parchment, each about 25 x 25 cm (10 x 10 inches). Put the spring onions and carrot in the centre of 2 of the pieces of parchment and top each with 2 of the sole rolls. Drizzle over the wine and sprinkle over the lemon rind. Season with salt and pepper. Put the other pieces of baking parchment on top and tightly roll up each side to make 2 parcels.

Transfer the parcels to a baking sheet and bake in a preheated oven, 200°C (400°F), Gas Mark 6, for about 20 minutes.

Meanwhile, cook the asparagus. Heat the butter and oil in a frying pan. Add the asparagus and fry for 2–3 minutes until just tender. Season to taste. Arrange the asparagus on warm serving plates and scatter over some Parmesan shavings. Add the fish parcels and serve.

For asparagus with tarragon & lemon dressing, make the dressing by mixing together 1 tablespoon tarragon vinegar, grated rind of ½ lemon, ¼ teaspoon Dijon mustard, a pinch of sugar, 1 tablespoon chopped tarragon and 2–3 tablespoons olive oil. Season to taste with salt and pepper. Heat 1 tablespoon olive oil in a frying pan. Add 250 g (8 oz) trimmed asparagus and cook for about 5 minutes, turning occasionally. Transfer to a shallow dish, pour over the dressing and allow to stand for 5 minutes.

oriental gingered salmon

Serves **2**

Preparation time **10 minutes**

Cooking time **6–10 minutes**

3–4 **spring onions**, shredded

1 cm (½ inch) piece of **fresh root ginger**, peeled and cut into strips

1 tablespoon **dry ginger ale** or **ginger cordial**

1 tablespoon **light soy sauce**

2 skinless **salmon fillets**, each about 125 g (4 oz)

Mix the spring onions, fresh ginger, ginger ale or cordial and soy sauce in a bowl.

Put the salmon in a covered frying pan and poach in the mixture for 3–5 minutes on each side. Top up with a little water if needed.

Garnish the salmon with the spring onions and ginger and pour over the remaining ginger ale mixture. Serve with steamed cabbage, mangetout and new potatoes, boiled in their skins.

For creamy peppered salmon, press 2 skinless salmon fillets into 1 tablespoon crushed peppercorns. Heat 1 tablespoon olive oil in a frying pan and cook the salmon for 2 minutes on each side until just cooked through. Add 4 tablespoons crème fraîche to the pan, cook gently to warm through and serve with new potatoes and steamed green vegetables.

pork with apricot & sage stuffing

Serves **2**

Preparation time **10 minutes**

Cooking time **20 minutes**

300 g (10 oz) **pork tenderloin**

1 tablespoon **olive oil**

1 small **onion**, finely sliced

6 ready-to-eat **dried apricots**, finely chopped

1 tablespoon **sage**, chopped

1 tablespoon **pine nuts**

fresh sage leaves, to garnish

Smashed beans

400 g (13 oz) can **cannellini beans**, rinsed and drained

1 **garlic clove**, sliced

100 ml (3½ fl oz) **chicken stock** (see page 146 for homemade)

2 tablespoons **crème fraîche**

salt and **black pepper**

Make a cut along the length of the tenderloin, taking care that you do not cut all the way through.

Heat half the oil in a nonstick pan. Add the onion and fry for 2–3 minutes until softened. Add the apricots, sage and pine nuts and cook for a further minute.

Spread the stuffing mixture along the length of the pork and secure with cocktail sticks or string.

Heat the remaining oil in a frying pan. Add the pork and fry for a few minutes until browned all over. Transfer it to a roasting tin and cook in a preheated oven, 200°C (400°F), Gas Mark 6, for 10–15 minutes or until just cooked through.

Meanwhile, put the beans, garlic and stock in a pan and simmer for 5 minutes. Add the crème fraîche and season to taste with salt and pepper. Mash the bean mixture with a potato masher and serve with the pork, garnished with the whole sage leaves.

For pork fillet with apricots, cut 350g (11½ oz) pork fillet into 6 slices. Cook the pork in a hot griddle pan for 7–8 minutes, transfer to an ovenproof dish and keep warm. Cut 1 red onion into wedges, keeping the root end intact. Cook on the griddle for about 5 minutes and add to the pork. Halve and stone 4 apricots and cook the halves on the griddle for 5 minutes on each side, adding a sprig of thyme for the last minute. Add the apricots and thyme to the pork. Mix together 2 tablespoons olive oil and 2 teaspoons cider vinegar and drizzle over the pork. Serve with boiled rice.

beef fillet with walnut pesto

Serves **2**
Preparation time **5 minutes**
Cooking time **5 minutes**

2 pieces of **beef fillet**, each
about 200 g (7 oz)
50 g (2 oz) **toasted walnuts**
3 tablespoons chopped mixed
herbs, such as coriander,
parsley and basil
2 tablespoons grated
Parmesan cheese
1 **garlic clove**
2 tablespoons **olive oil**
salt and **black pepper**

Heat a griddle or heavy-based frying pan. Season the
meat with salt and pepper, add to the pan and cook for
2 minutes on each side or until cooked to your liking.

Meanwhile, place the walnuts, herbs, Parmesan, garlic
and oil in a food processor or blender and process until
combined but still retaining a little texture.

Serve the cooked steaks with the sauce spooned on
top and accompanied with steamed new potatoes and
sugar snap peas.

For grilled vegetables with walnut pesto, make the
walnut pesto as above. Heat a griddle pan and cook a
halved and deseeded red pepper, a halved aubergine,
2 quartered red onions and 6 asparagus spears.
Serve the vegetables on a bed of steamed couscous
with the pesto.

stuffed mushrooms with tofu

Serves **2**
Preparation time **15 minutes**
Cooking time **18–20 minutes**

600 ml (1 pint) **boiling water**
2 teaspoons **vegetable stock powder**
4 large **portobello mushrooms**, stalks removed
2 tablespoons **olive oil**
75 g (3 oz) **red onion**, finely chopped
2 tablespoons **pine nuts**
250 g (8 oz) **tofu**, diced
½ teaspoon **cayenne pepper**
2 tablespoons chopped **basil**
50 g (2 oz) **Parmesan cheese**, finely grated
175 g (6 oz) **baby spinach leaves**
salt and **black pepper**

Pour the boiling water into a wide pan, then stir in the stock powder. Add the mushrooms, poach for 2–3 minutes, then remove and drain on kitchen paper.

Heat a little of the oil in a frying pan. Add the onion and fry gently until soft. Remove from the heat and allow to cool.

Dry-fry the pine nuts in a clean pan until golden-brown, remove from the heat, then combine with the onion, tofu, cayenne pepper, basil and remaining oil. Season to taste with salt and black pepper.

Sprinkle some grated Parmesan over each mushroom, then stuff the onion mixture into the mushrooms. Put them in a flameproof dish about 15 cm (6 inches) square below a preheated medium grill for about 10 minutes, until heated through and the cheese has melted.

Scatter the spinach leaves on 2 plates and arrange two hot mushrooms on top (the heat of the mushrooms will wilt the spinach).

For tofu & mushroom pasta, cook 300 g (10 oz) pasta in boiling water according to the instructions on the packet. Drain thoroughly. Meanwhile, slice 2 portobello mushrooms. Heat 1 tablespoon olive oil in a frying pan and fry the mushrooms with 40 g (1½ oz) chopped red onion. Add the mushrooms and onion to the pasta and add all the remaining ingredients above. Stir through 3 tablespoons double cream, warm gently and serve.

moroccan lamb with couscous

Serves **2**

Preparation time **10 minutes**, plus marinating

Cooking time **5 minutes**

4 **lamb cutlets** or 2 **lamb steaks**

2 teaspoons **ras el hanout**

grated rind and juice of ½ **lemon**

1 **garlic clove**, crushed

1 tablespoon **olive oil**

Couscous

300 ml (½ pint) boiling **chicken stock** (see page 146 for homemade)

150 g (5 oz) **couscous**

4 fresh or ready-to-eat dried **apricots**, chopped

50 g (2 oz) blanched and toasted **almonds**, roughly chopped

2 tablespoons chopped **fresh coriander**

salt and **black pepper**

Put the lamb in a non-metallic dish. Mix together the ras el hanout, lemon rind and juice, garlic and oil. Season to taste with salt and pepper and rub the mixture all over the lamb. Leave to marinate for at least 1 hour.

Cook the lamb under a preheated hot grill, turning once, for about 2 minutes each side, until it is browned and cooked to your liking.

Meanwhile, pour the boiling stock over the couscous, cover tightly and allow to absorb the liquid for 5 minutes. Fluff it up with a fork.

Toss the apricots and coriander through the couscous and serve with the lamb.

For couscous with grilled vegetables, mix 150 g (5 oz) couscous with 300 ml (½ pint) boiling vegetable stock. Chop 1 red pepper and ½ yellow pepper. Halve 3 small courgettes and cut 1 red onion into wedges. Put the vegetables in a roasting tin with 12 cherry tomatoes and 1 sliced garlic clove. Drizzle over 1 tablespoon olive oil and cook under a preheated hot grill, turning occasionally, for 5–6 minutes. Add 50 g (2 oz) trimmed asparagus to the tin and cook for a further 2–3 minutes. Fork the grated rind and juice of ½ lemon through the couscous and serve with the vegetables.

stilton soufflés

Serves **2**
Preparation time **10 minutes**
Cooking time **15 minutes**

15 g (½ oz) **butter**, plus extra
  for greasing
1 tablespoon grated
  Parmesan cheese
15 g (½ oz) **plain flour**
100 ml (3½ oz) **milk**
50 g (1¾ oz) **Stilton**,
  crumbled
1 **egg**, separated

Butter 2 ramekins, each holding 150 ml (¼ pint), and coat the bottom and sides with grated Parmesan.

Melt the butter in a small saucepan and add the flour. Whisk to make a smooth paste, then gradually add the milk, stirring all the time, until the sauce thickens. Allow to cool a little, then beat in the Stilton and egg yolk.

Whisk the egg white in a clean bowl until it forms soft peaks. Fold into the cheese mixture, then spoon into the prepared ramekins. Cook in a preheated oven, 200°C (400°F), Gas Mark 6, for about 15 minutes until golden and risen. Serve hot with watercress salad (see below) and some crusty, seeded bread.

For watercress & apple salad, to serve as an accompaniment, mix together in a small bowl 2 tablespoons lemon juice, ½ teaspoon Dijon mustard, 1 teaspoon clear honey and 1 tablespoon olive oil. Finely slice 1 apple and mix with 50 g (2 oz) watercress. Drizzle the dressing over the watercress and apple, toss and serve.

aubergine parcels with pine nuts

Serves **2**

Preparation time **30 minutes**, plus chilling

Cooking time **12–15 minutes**

1 tablespoon **pine nuts**

1 long, large **aubergine**

125 g (4 oz) **mozzarella cheese**

1 large or 2 small **plum tomatoes**

8 large **basil leaves**, plus extra, torn, to garnish

1 tablespoon **olive oil**

salt and **black pepper**

Tomato dressing

2 tablespoons **olive oil**

1 teaspoon **balsamic vinegar**

1 teaspoon **sun-dried tomato paste**

1 teaspoon **lemon juice**

Make the dressing. Whisk together the oil, vinegar, tomato paste and lemon juice in a small bowl. Set aside.

Dry-fry the pine nuts in a hot pan until golden brown. Set aside.

Cut the stalk off the aubergine and cut it lengthwise to give 8 slices (disregarding the ends). Put the slices in a pan of boiling salted water and cook for 2 minutes. Drain and dry on kitchen paper. Cut the mozzarella into 4 slices and the tomato into 8 slices (disregarding the outer edges).

Put 2 aubergine slices in an ovenproof dish, forming an X-shape. Put a slice of tomato on top, season with salt and pepper, add a basil leaf, a slice of mozzarella, another basil leaf, then more salt and pepper, and finally another slice of tomato. Fold the edges of the aubergine around the filling to make a parcel. Repeat with the other ingredients to make 4 parcels in total. Cover and chill in the refrigerator for 20 minutes.

Brush the aubergine parcels with oil. Put the dish under a preheated hot grill and cook for about 5 minutes on each side until golden-brown. Serve 2 parcels per person, drizzled with the dressing, and scattered with the pine nuts and torn basil leaves.

For aubergine parcels with garlic bruschetta, drizzle 4 slices of ciabatta with 1 tablespoon olive oil and rub with garlic. Toast until golden. Make aubergine parcels as above and place one on each slice, top with Parmesan shavings and scatter over 1 tablespoon toasted pine nuts.

smoked salmon & veg pasta

Serves **2**
Preparation time **10 minutes**
Cooking time **30 minutes**

1 **courgette**, chopped
1 **red pepper**, cored,
    deseeded and chopped
1 **red onion**, cut into thin
    wedges
2 **garlic cloves**, sliced
2 tablespoons **olive oil**
150 g (5 oz) **pasta shapes**
150 g (5 oz) **smoked salmon**
6 tablespoons **double cream**
grated rind and juice of
    ½ **lemon**
1 tablespoon **toasted**
    pine nuts
handful of **basil leaves**, torn

Put the courgette, red pepper, red onion and garlic in a roasting tin, drizzle over the oil and cook in a preheated oven, 220°C (425°F), Gas Mark 7, for 25–30 minutes until the vegetables are tender and beginning to char.

Meanwhile, cook the pasta in boiling water according to the instructions on the packet. Drain.

Cut the salmon into bite-sized pieces and mix with the cream, lemon rind and juice, pine nuts and torn basil leaves. Toss the cream sauce through the pasta, add the roasted vegetables and warm through gently before serving.

For feta & chorizo roast vegetable pasta, add 75 g (3 oz) sliced chorizo to the vegetables halfway through the cooking time and replace the salmon with 50 g (2 oz) crumbled feta cheese. Then toss the cream sauce through the pasta with the roasted vegetables, warming gently before serving.

tarragon chicken with potatoes

Serves **2**

Preparation time **10 minutes**, plus marinating

Cooking time **1 hour**

chicken breasts, each cut into about 8 slices

4 tablespoons **lemon juice**

1 **garlic clove**, crushed

handful of **tarragon**, chopped

25 g (1 oz) **butter**

125 g (4 oz) mixed **mushrooms**, sliced

200 ml (7 fl oz) **double cream**

salt and **black pepper**

Sliced potatoes

3 large unpeeled **potatoes**, thinly sliced

1 teaspoon finely chopped **thyme**

1 tablespoon **olive oil**

150 ml (¼ pint) **vegetable stock** (see page 94 for homemade)

5 g (¼ oz) **butter**

Layer the potato slices and thyme in a well-greased, ovenproof dish. Mix together the oil and stock and pour over the potatoes. Dot over the butter, cover with foil and bake in a preheated oven, 160°C (325°F), Gas Mark 3, for 1 hour, removing the foil halfway through cooking.

Meanwhile, put the chicken in a non-metallic dish. Mix together the lemon juice, garlic and tarragon, pour the mixture over the chicken and leave to marinate for 30 minutes.

Heat the butter in a frying pan and fry the mushrooms, then add the chicken and any juices and fry for a further 3 minutes. Add the cream to the pan and season with salt and pepper. Simmer gently for a couple of minutes until the chicken is just cooked. Serve with the potatoes and steamed green beans.

For tarragon chicken & mushroom pasta, cook 150 g (5 oz) pasta shapes in boiling water according to the instructions on the packet. Drain thoroughly. Cut the chicken into bite-sized pieces and cook as above. Toss the pasta through the chicken sauce together with 75 g (3 oz) rocket.

quail, sugar snaps & baby corn

Serves **2**

Preparation time **10 minutes**, plus marinating

Cooking time **about 12 minutes**

2 **quails**, partly boned

150 g (5 oz) **sugar snap peas**, halved

150 g (5 oz) **baby corn**, halved lengthways

1 **garlic clove**, crushed

1 tablespoon **vegetable oil**

2 teaspoons **sesame oil**

2 teaspoons **light soy sauce**

Marinade

1 small **shallot**, chopped

2.5 cm (1 inch) **fresh root ginger**, peeled and grated

1 tablespoon **pomegranate syrup**

1 tablespoon **sweet soy sauce**

1 tablespoon **brown rice vinegar**

½ tablespoon **tamarind paste**

1 teaspoon **five spice powder**

Spatchcock the quails, if your butcher has not done so, by removing the backbone, snipping off the wing tips and flattening the bird with the palm of your hand.

Make the marinade by mixing together all the ingredients in a large bowl. Add the quails and turn to coat, cover and leave in the refrigerator for at least 8 hours but preferably overnight.

Heat a heavy-based frying pan over a medium heat. Cook the quails for 8–10 minutes, turning once and basting regularly with the marinade. Once the quails are cooked through and sticky, remove them from the pan, cover with foil and keep warm.

Heat a clean, nonstick frying pan over a high heat. Toss the sugar snap peas and baby corn in a bowl with the garlic and vegetable oil and then pour into the frying pan. Cook quickly for 2 minutes, moving them occasionally so they don't stick. Return them to the bowl, toss with the sesame oil and soy sauce and serve immediately, topped with the sticky quail and any juices.

For tofu & pomegranate salad, halve 200 g (7 oz) tofu horizontally. Make the marinade as above, put the tofu in a non-metallic dish and cover with the marinade. Cover and refrigerate for at least 30 minutes. Heat a frying pan over a high heat and cook the tofu, turning once, for about 2 minutes. Meanwhile, prepare the salad as above, stir through the garlic, vegetable and sesame oils and soy sauce together with the seeds from a pomegranate. Serve with the cooked tofu.

tuna with tomato & herbs

Serves **2**
Preparation time **15 minutes**
Cooking time **25–35 minutes**

2 fresh **tuna steaks**, each
  about 125 g (5 oz)
1 large **garlic clove**, cut into
  fine slivers
2 teaspoons lightly ground
  coriander seeds
2 tablespoons finely chopped
  mint, plus extra to serve
2 teaspoons **capers**, drained
salt and **black pepper**

Tomato and herb sauce
2 tablespoons **olive oil**
1 large **garlic clove**, finely
  chopped
½ teaspoon crumbled dried
  red chilli (optional)
1 teaspoon dried **oregano**
2 tablespoons roughly
  chopped **mint**
4 tablespoons **dry white wine**
2 large **tomatoes**, skinned,
  deseeded and roughly
  chopped

Use a sharp knife to make small incisions in the tuna
steaks. Insert some garlic, coriander seeds and mint
into each opening.

Make the sauce. Heat a little of the oil in a saucepan,
add the garlic, chilli, oregano and any coriander seeds
remaining from the tuna. Cook, stirring, until the garlic
turns golden brown. Add the mint, wine and tomatoes
and cook over a medium heat for 5–10 minutes.

Heat the remaining oil in a small flameproof casserole on
the hob. Add the tuna and seal on both sides. Pour the
sauce over the tuna, season to taste with salt and pepper
and transfer the casserole to a preheated oven, 220°C
(425°F), Gas Mark 7, and cook for 15–20 minutes.

Sprinkle the baked tuna with a little mint and the
capers. Serve with new potatoes and steamed spinach,
spring greens or broccoli.

For tuna pasta bake, cook 175 g (6 oz) pasta
shapes in boiling water according to the instructions
on the packet. Drain and transfer to an ovenproof
dish. Flavour and cook the tuna and make the sauce
as above. Flake the tuna and spoon it and the sauce
over the pasta. Sprinkle over 4 tablespoons fresh
granary breadcrumbs and 2 tablespoons grated
Parmesan cheese. Cook under a preheated hot
grill for 1–2 minutes until golden.

tofu pad thai

Serves **2**
Preparation time **10 minutes**
Cooking time **5 minutes**

2 tablespoons **vegetable oil**
125 g (5 oz) **tofu**, cut into
  bite-sized pieces
2 **garlic cloves**, sliced
pinch of **chilli flakes**
bunch of **spring onions**,
  sliced
50 g (2 oz) **bean sprouts**
125 g (5 oz) **flat rice noodles**
2 **eggs**, beaten
3 tablespoons **fish sauce**
  (**nam pla**) optional
juice of **1 lime**
25 g (1 oz) roasted **salted**
  peanuts, roughly chopped
2 tablespoons chopped
  fresh coriander

Heat the oil in a wok or frying pan. Add the tofu and fry for 2 minutes, then add the garlic, chilli, spring onions and bean sprouts. Fry for a further minute.

Cook the noodles according to the instructions on the packet. Drain and add to the pan. Heat through, then stir in the eggs, fish sauce (if using) and lime juice and continue to cook, stirring, until the egg is cooked. Serve sprinkled with the peanuts and coriander.

For prawn pad thai, cook 125 g (5 oz) noodles according to the instructions on the packet. Fry the garlic, chilli flakes, spring onions, bean sprouts as above. Stir in the drained noodles and add 150 g (5 oz) cooked peeled prawns to the pan. Add the beaten eggs, fish sauce and lime juice, stirring until the eggs are cooked, and serve immediately.

scallop, rocket & pancetta linguini

Serves **2**
Preparation time **5 minutes**
Cooking time **10 minutes**

150 g (5 oz) **linguini**
1 tablespoon **olive oil**
100 g (3½ oz) **pancetta**,
   chopped
1 **garlic clove**, crushed
1 **red chilli**, chopped
   (optional)
8 **scallops**, halved
50 g (2 oz) **rocket leaves**

Cook the linguini according to the instructions on the packet. Drain.

Meanwhile, heat the oil in a frying pan. Add the pancetta and cook for a couple of minutes until it is beginning to brown, add the garlic and chilli (if using) and fry for a further minute. Add the scallops to the pan and cook for a further minute, turning halfway through cooking.

Toss the linguini with the rocket, add the scallops and serve immediately.

For monkfish pasta, cook 150 g (5 oz) pasta shapes according to the instructions on the packet. Cook the pancetta as above, and add a crushed garlic clove and a deseeded and chopped red chilli. Cut 200 g (7 oz) monkfish fillet into cubes and add to the pan, cooking for a further 2 minutes or until the fish is cooked through. Add the pasta to the pan, stir through to combine with the rocket leaves and serve.

mediterranean pork casserole

Serves **2**

Preparation time **10 minutes**

Cooking time **1 hour**

1 tablespoon **olive oil**

250 g (8 oz) **lean pork**, cubed

1 **red onion**, cut into thin
   wedges

1 **garlic clove**, crushed

1 **yellow pepper**, cored,
   deseeded and chopped

8 **artichoke hearts**, drained
   and quartered

200 g (7 oz) can **chopped
   tomatoes**

1 small glass **red wine**

50 g (2 oz) **black olives**

grated rind of 1 **lemon**

1 **bay leaf**

1 **thyme** spring, plus extra
   to garnish

Heat the oil in an ovenproof casserole. Add the pork
and fry for 2–3 minutes until browned all over. Remove
the pork from the casserole with a slotted spoon and
set aside.

Add the onion, garlic and yellow pepper to the
casserole and fry for 2 minutes. Return the pork to
the casserole together with the remaining ingredients.

Bring to the boil, cover and simmer for about an hour
or until the meat is tender. Garnish with thyme and
serve accompanied with garlic bread.

For borlotti bean casserole, cook the onion, garlic,
yellow pepper, artichoke hearts and tomatoes as above.
Rinse and drain 400 g (13 oz) can of borlotti beans and
add to the casserole with the wine, olives, lemon rind
and herbs. Bring to the boil and cook slowly for about
1 hour. Serve garnished with chopped parsley.

duck breast salad with orange

Serves **2**
Preparation time **15 minutes**
Cooking time **15–20 minutes**

2 boneless **duck breasts**
2 handfuls of mixed **rocket and watercress leaves**, chopped
2 **oranges**, peeled and segmented
salt and **black pepper**

Dressing
2 tablespoons **olive oil**
1 tablespoon **balsamic vinegar**
1 **garlic clove**, crushed
pinch of dry **mustard**
good pinch of **sugar**

Lay the duck breasts, skin side down, on a board, cover with clingfilm or greaseproof paper and using a rolling pin, bash them to flatten them slightly. Remove the clingfilm, turn the breasts over and score the skin diagonally or in a crisscross pattern with a very sharp knife. Rub the skin all over with salt.

Put the duck breasts, skin side up, on a rack in a roasting pan and cook in a preheated oven, 200°C (400°F), Gas Mark 6, for 15–20 minutes or until the duck is brown on the outside but a little pink in the middle.

Meanwhile, cut the skin off the oranges and cut into segments, working over a bowl to catch the juice. Add the orange juice to the ingredients for the dressing, season to taste with salt and pepper and stir well.

Transfer the cooked duck breasts onto a chopping board and slice them thinly on the diagonal. Put the chopped rocket and watercress leaves in the centre of 2 serving plates and arrange the duck slices and orange segments on top.

Whisk the dressing and spoon it over the salad.

For duck & noodle salad, cook 2 boneless duck breasts as above and cut into thick slices. Cook 100 g (3½ oz) egg noodles according to the instructions on the packet. Drain. In a bowl whisk together the juice of 1 orange, 1 teaspoon sesame oil and 1 teaspoon clear honey. Combine the noodles with the dressing and stir through 1 tablespoon sesame seeds, 100 g (3½ oz) blanched sugar snap peas, 2 segmented oranges and 2 sliced spring onions. Arrange the duck on the salad and serve.

desserts

ginger peaches & vanilla cream

Serves **2**

Preparation time **10 minutes**

Cooking time **15 minutes**

2 fresh **peaches**, halved and
stoned

1 piece **stem ginger**, finely
chopped

2 tablespoons **ginger syrup**

3 **ginger biscuits**, roughly
crushed

25 g (1 oz) **unsalted butter**,
melted

Cream

4 tablespoons **double cream**

seeds of **1 vanilla pod**

1 tablespoon **icing sugar**

Put the peaches, cut side, up in an ovenproof dish. Mix
together the ginger, syrup, biscuits and butter and
spoon over the peaches.

Cook in a preheated oven, 200°C (400°F), Gas Mark
6, for 12–15 minutes until bubbling and the peaches
are tender.

Whip together the cream with the vanilla seeds and
icing sugar until just stiff and serve with the peaches.

For almondy baked pears, halve and core 2 fresh
pears. Mix together 15 g (½ oz) melted butter and the
grated rind and juice 1 small orange. Cut 25 g (1 oz)
marzipan into 4 and use the pieces to fill the cavities
of the pears. Drizzle over the butter mixture and bake
in a preheated oven, 200°C (400°F), Gas Mark 6, for
12–15 minutes. Serve with crème fraîche and a
scattering of toasted flaked almonds.

vanilla cheesecakes & rhubarb

Makes **2**

Preparation time **10 minutes**, plus chilling

Base

3 **oat biscuits**, roughly crushed

15 g (½ oz) **unsalted butter**, melted

1 tablespoon toasted **hazelnuts**, chopped

Cheesecake

100 g (3½ oz) **cream cheese**

4 tablespoons **mascarpone cheese**

1 tablespoon **icing sugar**

few drops of **vanilla extract**

Rhubarb

4 sticks of **rhubarb**, chopped

2 tablespoons **caster sugar**

Make the bases. Mix together the biscuits, butter and hazelnuts and press the mixture into the base of 2 large ramekins or serving dishes. Chill for 10 minutes.

Beat together the cream cheese with the mascarpone, icing sugar and vanilla extract and spoon over the base. Chill for 10 minutes.

Meanwhile, put the rhubarb and sugar in a medium-sized pan and simmer gently until the rhubarb is tender. Allow to cool, then spoon over the cheesecake and serve.

For ginger & raspberry cheesecakes, make the bases with 3 crushed ginger biscuits, 15 g (½ oz) unsalted butter and 1 tablespoon chopped hazelnuts. Make the cheesecake as above and stir through 100 g (3½ oz) roughly crushed raspberries. Before serving scatter a few more whole raspberries on top together with 1 tablespoon grated plain dark chocolate.

pear pancakes

Serves **2**
Preparation time **10 minutes**
Cooking time **20 minutes**

25 g (1 oz) **unsalted butter**,
  melted
25 g (1 oz) **self-raising flour**
25 g (1 oz) **wholemeal**
  self-raising flour
15 g (½ oz) **oatmeal**
½ tablespoon **caster sugar**
1 **egg**, lightly beaten
150 ml (¼ pint) **buttermilk**
milk, for thinning (optional)
vegetable oil, for brushing
3 **pears**, peeled, cored and
  chopped
pinch of **cinnamon**
1 tablespoon **water**

Mix together the butter, flours, oatmeal, sugar, egg and buttermilk to make a smooth batter, adding a little extra milk if the mixture looks very thick.

Brush a nonstick frying pan with a little oil and heat. Add a ladleful of batter to the pan and cook for 2 minutes on each side until golden. Remove the pancake from the pan and keep warm. Repeat with the remaining batter mixture to make 6 small pancakes in total.

Meanwhile, put the pears and cinnamon in a small saucepan with the water. Cover and cook gently for 2–3 minutes until just tender. Serve the pancakes with the cooked pears.

For blackberry & almond pancakes, make the pancakes as above. Put 150 g (5 oz) blackberries in a saucepan and add 1 tablespoon water and 1 tablespoon caster sugar. Heat, stirring, until softened. Spoon the mixture over the pancakes, scatter over 1 tablespoon toasted almonds and serve.

honey roast figs

Serves **2**
Preparation time **5 minutes**
Cooking time **20 minutes**

6 ripe fresh **figs**
1 tablespoon **clear honey**
grated rind and juice **1 orange**
pinch of **ground cinnamon**
2 tablespoons **crème fraîche**
1 tablespoon chopped **mint**

Cut a deep cross in each fig and place them in an ovenproof dish.

Mix together the honey, orange rind and juice and cinnamon and pour over the figs. Cook in a preheated oven, 190°C (375°F), Gas Mark 5, for about 20 minutes or until bubbling and the figs are squidgy.

Mix together the crème fraîche and mint and serve with the figs.

For honey mascarpone figs with raspberries, cut a deep cross in 6 figs and place them in a serving dish. Mix together 2 tablespoons mascarpone cheese with 1 tablespoon clear honey and spoon the mixture into the figs. Put 150 g (5 oz) raspberries in a small pan with 1 teaspoon icing sugar and cook, stirring, over a low heat until the raspberries are beginning to soften. Serve with the figs.

yogurt with berry coulis

Serves **2**

Preparation time **5 minutes**, plus chilling

6 tablespoons **double cream**
6 tablespoons **natural yogurt**
75 g (3 oz) **blueberries**
75 g (3 oz) **raspberries**
3 tablespoons **caster sugar**
2 tablespoons **dark brown sugar**

Put the cream and yogurt in a bowl and whip together until just firm.

Put the blueberries and raspberries in a small saucepan. Cook over a low heat for 5–6 minutes until the juices start to ooze. Process with a hand blender or push through a sieve.

Stir the cream mixture into the fruit and spoon into 2 individual ramekins or glasses. Sprinkle over the dark brown sugar and chill in the refrigerator for 15 minutes until the sugar has dissolved on the top. Serve.

For yogurt with tropical fruit coulis, mix together 6 tablespoons each of double cream and natural yogurt. Blend together the flesh of 1 ripe mango and 1 passion fruit. Stir through the yogurt mixture and top with dark brown sugar as above. Chill for 15 minutes before serving.

pineapple panettone

Serves **2**

Preparation time **4 minutes**

Cooking time **2–3 minutes**

4 **pineapple rings** in juice,
   drained

4 slices of **panettone**

50 g (2 oz) **mini
   marshmallows**

25 g (1 oz) **macadamia nuts**,
   crushed

2 tablespoons **vanilla sugar**

icing sugar, to dust

Pat the pineapple rings dry on paper towels and arrange them on 2 slices of panettone. Scatter over the marshmallows and crushed macadamia nuts and sprinkle with the vanilla sugar. Top with the remaining 2 slices of panettone.

Toast in a sandwich grill for 2–3 minutes or according to the manufacturer's instructions until the bread is golden and the marshmallows are beginning to melt. Slice each sandwich into small rectangles and dust with icing sugar. Serve immediately.

For mango & almond panettone, replace the pineapple rings with 4 slices of mango. Scatter over 50 g (2 oz) mini-marshmallows and 50 g (2 oz) flaked almonds and toast as above.

baked chocolate cheesecake

Serves **2**

Preparation time **10 minutes**, plus cooling

Cooking time **45 minutes**

25 g (1 oz) **unsalted butter**, melted

75 g (3 oz) **ratafia biscuits**, crushed

150 g (5 oz) **cream cheese**

25 g (1 oz) **caster sugar**

50 g (2 oz) **mascarpone cheese**

50 g (2 oz) **dark plain chocolate**, melted

1 **egg**

1 **egg yolk**

To decorate
crème fraîche
chocolate shavings

Melt the butter in a saucepan. Add the crushed biscuits and mix well. Divide the mixture between two tart tins, 10 cm (4 inches) across, and press down to form the cheesecake bases.

Place the cream cheese, caster sugar, mascarpone and chocolate in a small pan and warm over a gentle heat, stirring until the mixture is melted and blended.

Remove from the heat, allow to cool and then beat in the egg and the yolk.

Divide the chocolate mixture between the two tart tins, place them on a baking sheet and cook in a preheated oven, 180°C (350°F), Gas Mark 4, for 45 minutes or until set. Remove from the oven and leave the cheesecakes to cool before transferring them to the refrigerator. Chill until required, then decorate with a dollop of crème fraîche and chocolate shavings.

For white chocolate & raspberry cheesecake, make the base as above. Mix together the cream cheese, caster sugar and mascarpone as above, but using 50 g (2 oz) melted white chocolate instead of the dark chocolate. Allow to cool, beat in the egg and egg yolk, and stir 50 g (2 oz) raspberries through the mixture. Bake as above.

italian rice pudding

Serves **2**

Preparation time **10 minutes**, plus infusing

Cooking time **25 minutes**

25 g (1 oz) **raisins**
2 tablespoons **Marsala**
1 vanilla pod
300 ml (½ pint) **milk**
1–2 tablespoons **caster sugar**
finely grated rind of ½ **orange**, plus extra for decorating
¼ teaspoon **ground cinnamon**
50 g (2 oz) **risotto rice**
50 ml (2 fl oz) **double cream**
toasted flaked **almonds**, to decorate

Put the raisins and Marsala in a bowl and leave to soak.

Use the tip of a small, sharp knife to score the vanilla pod lengthways through to the centre. Put it in a heavy-based saucepan with the milk, bring just to the boil, then remove from the heat and leave to infuse for 20 minutes.

Stir the sugar, orange rind and cinnamon into the milk and return the pan to the heat. Tip in the rice and cook very gently, stirring frequently, for about 15 minutes until the mixture is thick and creamy and the rice is tender.

Stir in the steeped raisins and cream and heat gently for a further 2 minutes. Serve warm, decorated with flaked almonds and grated orange rind.

For crunchy brûlée rice pudding, spoon the cooked rice pudding into 2 ramekins or small, ovenproof dishes. Sprinkle 1 tablespoon demerara sugar over the top of each and cook under a preheated hot grill until the sugar has dissolved and is bubbling. Leave to cool until the sugar has hardened, and then serve.

walnut toast & fruit compôte

Serves **2**

Preparation time **5 minutes**, plus infusing

Cooking time **5 minutes**

Compôte

150 g (5 oz) mixed dried **fruit**, such as apricots, figs and prunes

150 ml (¼ pint) **apple juice**

150 ml (¼ pint) strong **black tea**

1 **star anise**

1 **cinnamon stick**

Toast

15 g (½ oz) **unsalted butter**

good pinch of **ground cinnamon**

2 slices of **walnut bread**

1 tablespoon **caster sugar**

Put the dried fruit, apple juice, tea, star anise and cinnamon stick in a small saucepan and bring to the boil. Remove the pan from the heat and set aside for 20 minutes.

Mix together the butter and cinnamon and spread half over 1 side of each slice of bread. Put the bread on a foil-lined baking sheet under a preheated hot grill and cook for 1–2 minutes until golden. Repeat with the other side.

Serve the toast with the cooled compôte and a scoop of vanilla ice cream.

For walnut toast & mixed berries, put 250 g (8 oz) frozen mixed berries in a saucepan with 1 tablespoon icing sugar and, if liked, a drizzle of crème de cassis. Cook over a medium heat until defrosted and the juices are oozing. Prepare the toast as above. Serve the berries on the toasts with ice cream.

cherry clafoutis

Serves **2**

Preparation time **5 minutes**
Cooking time **30 minutes**

250 g (8 oz) **cherries**, stoned
200 ml (7 fl oz) **full-fat milk**
3 tablespoons **single cream**
few drops of **vanilla extract**
2 eggs
50 g (2 oz) **caster sugar**
25 g (1 oz) **plain flour**
1 tablespoon roughly chopped
  blanched **almonds**
icing sugar, to dust

Butter a medium-sized ovenproof dish and put the cherries in it. Heat the milk, cream and vanilla extract in a small pan.

Whisk together the eggs and sugar until light and fluffy, then stir in the flour. Gradually stir in the heated milk, then pour this batter mix over the cherries and scatter the almonds over the top.

Bake in a preheated oven, 190°C (375°F), Gas Mark 5, for 25–30 minutes until golden and puffy. Serve with crème fraîche, if liked.

For plum clafoutis, halve and stone 4 ripe plums and place them in an ovenproof dish. Make the batter as above, pour it over the plums and cook in a preheated oven, 190°C (375°F), Gas Mark 5, for 25–30 minutes. Serve with ice cream.

chocolate & orange mousse

Serves **2**

Preparation time **10 minutes**, plus chilling

75 g (3 oz) **plain dark chocolate**

grated rind and juice of ½ **orange**, plus extra rind to decorate

2 tablespoons **double cream**

1 **egg**, separated

1 tablespoon **caster sugar**

Put the chocolate, orange rind and juice and cream in a small bowl over a pan of gently simmering water and heat gently until the chocolate has melted. Leave to cool, then beat in the egg yolk.

Meanwhile, whisk the egg white until it forms soft peaks, add the sugar and whisk until stiff.

Gently fold the egg white into the chocolate mixture, then spoon into glasses or ramekins. Chill for about 1 hour and decorate with orange rind before serving.

For minty choc pots, melt 75 g (3 oz) chocolate with 6 after-dinner chocolate mints and 2 tablespoons double cream. Continue as above, but before spooning the mixture into 2 serving dishes fold through 4 finely chopped mint and chocolate sticks.

toffee bananas & vanilla cream

Serves **2**
Preparation time **5 minutes**
Cooking time **5 minutes**

25 g (1 oz) **unsalted butter**
2 tablespoons dark **soft
  brown sugar**
2 large **bananas**, sliced
8 tablespoons **double cream**
1 teaspoon **rum**

Vanilla cream
4 tablespoons **double cream**
few drops of **vanilla extract**

Put the butter and sugar in a nonstick frying pan. Heat gently until the sugar has melted. Add the bananas and toss in the sauce for 1–2 minutes until warm and soft. Add the cream and rum and heat through.

Make the vanilla cream by whipping the cream and vanilla extract until just light and beginning to hold its shape. Serve with the bananas and drizzle with toffee sauce, if liked.

For toffee pineapple, melt 25 g (1 oz) unsalted butter with 2 tablespoons soft brown sugar in a frying pan. Add 2 thick slices of fresh pineapple, skinned and cored, and cook, turning once, for 2–3 minutes. Add 2 tablespoons single cream and 1 teaspoon rum. Serve with vanilla cream or ice cream.

lavender syllabub

Serves **2**

Preparation time **15 minutes**, plus infusing

1 tablespoon **caster sugar**
12 **lavender heads** or a few drops lavender cooking essence, **plus extra lavender heads to decorate**
100 ml (3½ fl oz) **medium white wine**
150 ml (¼ pint) **double cream**

Put the sugar, lavender heads and wine in a small saucepan, heat gently until the sugar has dissolved, then leave to stand for 10 minutes to allow the flavour to develop.

Strain the mixture, then add the cream and whip until it forms soft peaks. Transfer to serving glasses and chill. Serve each syllabub decorated with a lavender head if liked.

For orange syllabub, put 1 tablespoon caster sugar and the grated rind and juice of 1 orange into a small saucepan with 100 ml (3½ fl oz) white wine. Cook gently until the sugar has dissolved, then proceed as above.

plums in wine

Serves **2**
Preparation time **5 minutes**
Cooking time **10 minutes**

300 ml (½ pint) **white wine**
125 g (4 oz) **caster sugar**
grated rind and juice of
  1 **orange**
1 **star anise**
2 **cardamom pods**
6 fresh **plums**
1 tablespoon chopped
  pistachios

Put the wine, sugar, orange rind and juice, star anise and cardamom pods in a medium saucepan. Heat gently until the sugar has dissolved.

Add the plums to the wine mixture and simmer for 5–8 minutes or until tender. Remove the plums from the pan and divide between 2 dessert dishes.

Boil the wine mixture until it has reduced to a syrupy consistency. Pour it over the plums and scatter over the pistachios. Serve with crème fraîche or ice cream, if liked.

For pears in wine, heat 300 ml (½ pint) red wine with the sugar, orange rind and juice, star anise and cardamom pods as above. Peel 2 pears, add them to the saucepan and simmer 10 minutes. Transfer the pears to 2 dessert dishes and reduce the wine mixture to a syrup. Pour the syrup over the pears and scatter over 1 tablespoon flaked, toasted almonds. Serve with cream.

pecans, berries & ice cream

Serves **2**
Preparation time **20 minutes**
Cooking time **5 minutes**

50 g (2 oz) **pecan nuts**
2 tablespoons **caster sugar**
5 g (¼ oz) **unsalted butter**
250 g (8 oz) mixed **berries**,
  such as blackberries,
  raspberries and strawberries

Vanilla ice cream
1 **vanilla pod**
300 ml (½ pint) **double
  cream**
1 tablespoon **caster sugar**
2 **egg yolks**

Make the ice cream. Split the vanilla pod lengthways and scrape out the seeds. Put them in a medium saucepan with the cream and the sugar and heat to dissolve the sugar.

Whisk the egg yolks in a bowl. Whisking continually, pour the cream mixture over the yolks, return to the pan and heat gently, without allowing the mixture to boil, until just thickened. Transfer to a freezer-proof container and freeze.

Put the nuts, sugar and butter in a small saucepan and cook for 1–2 minutes, stirring, until the sugar has caramelised. Remove from the heat stir in the berries, then tip the mixture on to some greaseproof paper. When it is cold tap with a rolling pin to break into pieces. Serve the ice cream with the pecans and mixed berries.

For caramel pecan ice cream, make the pecan caramel as above. Fold together 300 ml (½ pint) fresh custard and 4 tablespoons whipped cream and a few drops vanilla extract. Fold in the pieces of pecan caramel, then transfer to a freezer-proof container and freeze until solid.

chocolate & hazelnut meringues

Serves **2**

Preparation time **10 minutes**

Cooking time **1 hour**, plus
cooling

Meringues

2 **egg whites**

100 g (3½ oz) **caster sugar**

50 g (2 oz) toasted
hazelnuts, chopped

50 g (2 oz) **dark plain
chocolate**, coarsely grated

Filling

100 ml (3½ fl oz) **whipping
cream**

1 tablespoon **caster sugar**

Put the egg whites in a clean bowl and whisk until
soft peaks form. Keep whisking and add the sugar a
spoonful at a time. Fold in half of the nuts and half of
the chocolate.

Spoon 8 spoonfuls on a lined baking sheet and
sprinkle with the remaining nuts. Cook in a preheated
oven, 140°C (275°F), Gas Mark 1, for about 1 hour.
Turn off the oven and leave the meringues in the oven
until they are cold.

Whip the cream and sugar to form soft peaks. Melt
the remaining chocolate and fold it into the cream to
create a marble effect. Use the chocolate cream to
sandwich 2 meringues together and serve.

For blueberry & raspberry meringue, use the
meringue ingredients above to make 1 large nest.
Cook and allow to cool as above. Fill the meringue
nest with the cream mixture and top with 200 g (7 oz)
fresh mixed blueberries and raspberries. Dust with
icing sugar and cocoa powder before serving.

summer fruit slush

Serves **2**
Preparation time **5 minutes**

about 375 g (12 oz) **summer
fruits**, such as strawberries,
raspberries, redcurrants
and blackberries, plus extra
to decorate
about 5 tablespoons **vanilla
syrup**, plus extra to serve
(optional)
crushed ice

Hull the strawberries (if necessary) and blend the
fruit in a food processor or blender until completely
smooth. Remove the seeds by straining the purée
through a non-metallic strainer into a large jug. Stir
in the vanilla syrup.

Fill 2 tall, narrow drinking glasses or sundae glasses
with crushed ice and pour in the vanilla-flavoured
fruit mixture.

Pile extra fruits on top of the drinks. Serve with long
spoons and extra syrup, if liked, for stirring in.

For tropical fruit slush, combine about 450 g
(14½ oz) mixed tropical fruits, such as mango,
kiwifruit and pineapple. Continue as above.

index

acknowledgements

Executive Editor: Nicola Hill
Editor: Amy Corbett
Design Manager: Tokiko Morishima
Designer: Nicola Liddiard, Nimbus Design
Photographer: Stephen Conroy
Home Economist: Emma Jane Frost
Props Stylist: Liz Hippisley
Production Controller: Carolin Stransky

Special photography: © Octopus Publishing
Group Ltd/Stephen Conroy.
Other photography: © Octopus Publishing Group
Ltd/Eleanor Skans 17, 153, 173; /Frank Adam
36, 82, 129, 145, 175, 181, 189; /Gareth
Sambridge 52, 55, 95, 99, 205, 215, 233; /Lis
Parsons 13, 18, 21, 23, 33, 61, 88, 107, 139;
/Stephen Conroy 8; /Will Heap 39, 45, 69, 74;
117, 169, 198.